Praise for *Don't Call It Quits*

Anyone thinking about making a career move should first read *Don't Call It Quits*—a practical guide to mapping out career options, even if it means staying in a current role. Shana invites us to "bring our human" to our professional choices by considering our values, purpose, and development goals.

—**Erica Keswin**, workplace strategist and bestselling author of *Bring Your Human to Work* and *Rituals Roadmap*

Taking control of your career doesn't require walking out the door. In this encouraging and helpful guide, Shana shows how to turn the job you have into a job that actually works for you.

—**Laura Vanderkam**, author of *The New Corner Office* and *168 Hours*

One of my favorite business books of the year: a brilliant guide to upgrading our careers without even changing jobs!

—**Tomas Chamorro-Premuzic**, psychology professor at Columbia University and author of *Why Do So Many Incompetent Men Become Leaders?*

If you want to reinvent your career, you don't have to leave your job. In this pragmatic and essential new book, Shana shows you how to empower yourself professionally and craft the job and career you want.

—**Dorie Clark**, *Wall Street Journal* bestselling author of *The Long Game* and *Reinventing You*, and executive education faculty, Duke University Fuqua School of Business

This is a highly actionable book, full of great stories about people just like you, people who figure out that they are more than just their job. People who demand meaning and purpose in the work they do, and use happiness and engagement as their North Star for good work. Read this book, change your mind, and design the job you love.

—**Bill Burnett**, coauthor of *Designing Your Life* and *Designing Your New Work Life* and executive director of the Life Design Lab at Stanford

When it comes to your work life, you probably have more options than you think," says Shana. But options can feel overwhelming, and Shana is here to guide you. This book comes at the perfect time. Whether you're thinking of leaving your job or facing a crossroads in your career, this book will help.

—**Morra Aarons-Mele**, author of *Hiding in the Bathroom* and host of the Anxious Achiever podcast

If you find yourself in a career rut, *Don't Call it Quits* can give you the insights, perspective, and sage advice not only to get you out of it, but also to take your career to new heights.

—**Dane Holmes**, CEO and cofounder of Eskalera and former global head of human capital management at Goldman Sachs

We're entering a new era where employees have much more agency about how, where, and when they work. This coincides with workers around the world thinking more about their why than ever before as the tumult of the world around is changing everything. What a perfect time for this book. Shana masterfully illustrates how employees can wield this power and take charge of their careers. It's never been more important for employees to take ownership of their careers. This book is an indispensable guide in showing you how to do just that.

—**Lars Schmidt**, author of *Redefining HR* and founder of Amplify

Shana has written a must-read! She offers clear, easy-to-follow advice; relatable stories; and just the right amount of "kick in the pants" to get you moving! What's more, she upends traditional wisdom that the only way to build a career you want is to leave, and instead takes the reader on a journey to illuminate their needs, values, and priorities—and then put that knowledge into action. Strongly recommend!

—**Kathryn Minshew**, founder and CEO of The Muse and author of *The New Rules of Work*

DON’T CALL IT

DON'T CALL IT

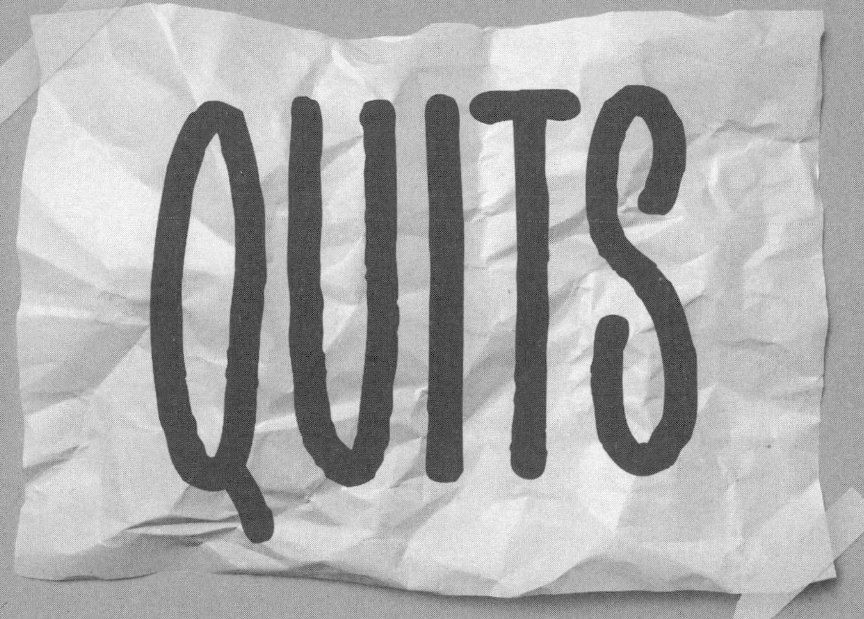

TURN THE JOB YOU HAVE INTO THE JOB YOU LOVE

SHANA LEBOWITZ GAYNOR

NEW YORK CHICAGO SAN FRANCISCO ATHENS LONDON
MADRID MEXICO CITY MILAN NEW DELHI
SINGAPORE SYDNEY TORONTO

1 2 3 4 5 6 7 8 9 LCR 27 26 25 24 23 22

ISBN 978-1-264-28524-2
MHID 1-264-28524-8

e-ISBN 978-1-264-28525-9
e-MHID 1-264-28525-6

Library of Congress Cataloging-in-Publication Data

Names: Gaynor, Shana Lebowitz, author.
Title: Don't call it quits : turn the job you have into the job you love / Shana Lebowitz Gaynor.
Description: New York : McGraw Hill, [2022] | Includes bibliographical references and index.
Identifiers: LCCN 2022014759 (print) | LCCN 2022014760 (ebook) | ISBN 9781264285242 (hardback) | ISBN 9781264285259 (ebook)
Subjects: LCSH: Job satisfaction. | Quality of work life. | Career changes.
Classification: LCC HF5549.5.J63 G39 2022 (print) | LCC HF5549.5.J63 (ebook) | DDC 306.3/61—dc23/eng/20220330
LC record available at https://lccn.loc.gov/2022014759
LC ebook record available at https://lccn.loc.gov/2022014760

McGraw Hill books are available at special quantity discounts to use as premiums and sales promotions or for use in corporate training programs. To contact a representative, please visit the Contact Us pages at www.mhprofessional.com.

McGraw Hill is committed to making our products accessible to all learners. To learn more about the available support and accommodations we offer, please contact us at accessibility@mheducation.com. We also participate in the Access Text Network (www.accesstext.org), and ATN members may submit requests through ATN.

To Eli, my greatest joy

CONTENTS

Part Three
GIVE YOURSELF OTHER OPTIONS

PREFACE

A few years ago, I almost left my job at *Insider*. In retrospect, it's easy to say this would have been a ridiculous idea and to remember all the wonderful, redeeming aspects of my work experience at that time. But I know I must have been feeling frustrated, confused, and stuck—like so many people reading this book right now—so I'm trying to get back in touch with some of those feelings and to remember what prompted me to look elsewhere.

At the time, my title was reporter, and I wrote about self-improvement, especially as it related to work and careers. For the most part, my job was interesting and a lot of fun. I read books about productivity and time management and distilled the most compelling takeaways into short articles. I wrote about my experience adopting the daily routines of successful and powerful people like Tim Ferris and Donald Trump. (*Spoiler:* Waking up at 5 a.m. to watch the news à la Trump is decidedly not for me. But getting to work at 11 a.m. after slowly drinking tea and meditating à la Ferris really could be.)

I was also responsible for publishing slideshows featuring signs that you're likable or that your relationship is strong. *Insider* published many slideshows in this vein; they were clever and appealed to readers' curiosity about themselves and how they fit into the world around them. Lately, though, I'd been dedicating much of my time and energy to these kinds of slideshows, often at the expense of digging deeper into the topics. And while these slideshows had once drawn tons of eyeballs, some readers seemed to have lost interest in this kind of content—meaning I was publishing tons of stories I didn't always enjoy writing *and* that fewer people were reading. Editorial leadership, however, still found value in these stories and continued assigning them. I'd grudgingly accept even when I would have preferred not to.

All this was happening shortly after I'd gotten married. I remember one evening when my husband was in the shower; from outside the bathroom door. I explained to him that I'd rather write more in-depth stories, say, features about entrepreneurship or analyses of new research on gender dynamics at work.

Shouting over the running water, I explained that these stories would make better use of my own curiosity and my interest in making readers think differently about their lives and careers. My husband listened patiently and murmured his agreement, but mostly it was me ranting and raving as I paced the narrow hallway.

Now that the harried months of choosing caterers and bands and bouquets were behind me, I had a little more energy and space on my calendar. So I applied for a couple of different roles elsewhere and set up some networking coffees with acquaintances who worked at places I'd like to write for. Nothing ended up panning out—but it was around that time that things changed for me at work.

A reporter on my team interviewed an executive about her favorite interview questions, one of which was, "What are the best and worst parts of your current job?" The woman who was my editor at the time is an exceptionally curious and compassionate person, and after publishing that reporter's story, she messaged everyone she managed, asking each of us to describe the best and worst parts of *our* job at *Insider*.

It was easy for me to tell her about the best parts of my job—things like sifting through psychological research and teasing out the most compelling parts to help readers improve their daily lives. But I remember my hands hovering over the keyboard, and my typing sentences and immediately deleting them, wondering how honest to be about the kind of assignments I'd prefer.

Ultimately, I wrote two sentences noting that I didn't always enjoy publishing those "signs" slideshows because they only skimmed the surface of important topics and that readers might not be crazy about them either. My editor wrote back almost immediately: She'd take these comments into account when generating assignments. Reader, I never published another one of those slideshows again.

Now this situation could have worked out much differently for me. Maybe I would have landed one of the jobs I'd applied for before my editor even had a chance to ask these questions. Or if I'd had a different type of editor, maybe she wouldn't have asked these questions at all, and I'd never have articulated my concerns, meaning I'd have stayed annoyed and resentful for a while. Or maybe the assignments I was resisting would have been critical to my job, and I'd have had to choose between doing them and leaving. In many ways, I was lucky.

What's clear to me now is that there are so many more productive ways I could have approached my own discontent. The rest of this book is dedicated to exploring these strategies and others, so that readers who feel similarly stymied can start to see a path out and make smart decisions about their lives and careers.

INTRODUCTION

THE CAREER QUESTION ON EVERYONE'S MIND

It took me three years as a careers reporter to crack the code.

After countless stories advising readers how to earn a plum promotion, manage a team for the first time, and ask their boss for help without looking foolish, I'd pinpointed the question people *really* wanted answers to.

SHOULD I QUIT MY JOB?

At *Insider*, the digital media outlet where I still work, I had access to real-time data on how many people were reading my articles. All I had to do was look up at the Chartbeat app displayed on the big-screen television above my desk, in the corner of the eighth floor of a shiny office building in New York City's Financial District.

Every time I published a story on deciding to quit, I'd watch those Chartbeat numbers creep higher and higher. Evidently there were a lot of professionals who felt frustrated in their jobs and wanted a way out. Some of them were, in all likelihood, members of the black- and gray-clad crowds I could see rushing to and from work on Liberty Street whenever I took a break to stare out the window.

In an effort to sate readers' appetites (and yes, to see that traffic surge), I started publishing more stories on quitting, and on related issues like what to do if you're miserable at work and how to know whether you're finally ready to pursue something entrepreneurial.

It wasn't just the bump in readership I enjoyed. I loved the way people's voices changed when they described the moment they decided to leave their six-figure consulting job or start their own business or go back to school and get their master's degree in education. Some people got quiet and reflective. Others perked up and talked breathlessly about the color-coded spreadsheet that helped them make the transition. Always, it was as though they were newly delighted to learn that it was possible to take control of their career trajectory.

Then, about a year after discovering this formula for blockbuster-hit articles, I got the sense that maybe I was doing readers a disservice. I remember walking from my office to the subway early one evening and wondering if I'd been perpetuating a form of "quitting porn." Was I playing into people's secret fantasies about upending their life and doing something totally new, encouraging them to think that these daydreams could become reality if only they wanted them badly enough? If so, I felt somewhat ashamed.

Because while giving your two weeks' notice can be liberating, it's not always the most practical move.

In reality, career transitions often require significant mental, emotional, and financial bandwidth. Some of us don't have that capacity at the moment. If you're supporting a young family, or you have student loans to pay off, or you work 12 hours a day and by the time you come home you're too exhausted to start identifying your core skills and passions, a major life overhaul might not be in the cards. Telling people they can take a big leap is asking them to buy into an admittedly tantalizing fantasy.

Especially when there are simpler paths to job satisfaction.

Looking back through interviews I'd conducted with organizational psychologists and influential business leaders, I realized that enjoying your job isn't a black-and-white issue: It's not a case of either you stick around and suck it up, or you leave and try to find something better. When it comes to your work life, you probably have more options than you think. There's a vast middle ground between those two extremes, where you keep your day job and make small-scale changes that help you feel a whole lot better about work.

In fact, you can generally use these strategies without your boss's input or permission. You might, for example, try shifting your mindset around meaningful work. Even if you're not a surgeon saving lives, helping your clients get their work done faster is no small thing. You might take up a hobby as a way to broaden your identity beyond the scope of your day job. Or you might simply stop beating yourself up for holding onto an unfulfilling gig that allows you to provide for your kids. These are just some of the strategies that career experts recommend and that the working professionals I've interviewed use to their advantage.

The important piece is being able to see possibility ahead of you. Just knowing that you have options—beyond staying or leaving—can be empowering. You'll feel less stuck because you'll know that your job satisfaction is largely up to you, as opposed to your boss or the vicissitudes of the global economy. You have agency within your own career, even if you don't yet recognize it.

I've been inching toward this book since the day I joined the *Insider* newsroom in 2015, though I didn't know it then. Over the past seven years I've interviewed academics, clinical psychologists, career coaches, and longtime executives about the best ways to build a successful work life. I've learned about the importance of things like growth mindset, managing up, and mapping out your transferable skills. I've also spoken with dozens of professionals across industries about the career development strategies that have, and haven't, worked for them.

While readers were devouring the stories I wrote on quitting, I realized people needed to understand all their options for feeling happier at work.

One thing I've learned on this beat is that absolutely everyone has a story about their career. Maybe they chose their current line of work out of necessity, but their true passion lies elsewhere. Maybe they took a menial job expecting to stay for months and ended up staying for decades. Maybe they started a business, watched it bomb, and reentered the corporate world, though secretly they'd like to try again. For each of these individuals, there's a path to greater happiness at work, no matter how out of reach it may seem. Even if they don't wind up crafting the perfect job, they'll be able to discern what about their work experience is within their locus of control and how they can make it better.

I have a career story, too. (Writing about the workplace doesn't necessarily make you smarter about your own career choices.) I've stayed too long in a job that wasn't working out; I've lost a job I cherished due to financial constraints on the company. I've also come close to making rash decisions while working at *Insider*—an organization that I love and that has supported my steady growth as a journalist—because things weren't going exactly as I would have liked.

In a way, this book is filled with the insights and advice that could have helped me at all these different junctures in my career. Mostly this book would have helped me see that I had the power to reshape my own work experience—and that the reshaping process could actually be pretty easy.

It can be easy for you, too.

A USER'S GUIDE TO THIS BOOK

Each chapter in this book will challenge your thinking around a different aspect of your work life. I've divided the book into three parts:

- **Part One.** Evaluate and Reevaluate (Chapters 1 through 4)
- **Part Two.** Take Action (Chapters 5 through 8)
- **Part Three.** Give Yourself Other Options (Chapters 9 through 12)

In Part One, you'll consider the benefits of sticking around when everyone else is jumping ship, ask yourself whether quitting is the best way to get what you want, learn to recognize when you're being influenced by cultural narratives about work, clarify what's going well in your career and what isn't, and come up with a personal definition of "meaning."

In Part Two, you'll consider different ways in which passion for work can manifest, start tackling the small stuff about your job that drives you crazy, tailor your role to what you really care about, and zero in on your own learning and development.

In Part Three, you'll map out ways in which your employer can promote your career development, identify other sources of fulfillment in your life besides work, make a plan for cautiously transitioning to entrepreneurship, and test the decision to quit using a series of expert-approved frameworks.

Each chapter concludes with a "Remember This" recap and with what I call a "Try This" exercise, which is designed to help you apply the ideas discussed in the chapter to your own situation.

I hope you read all 12 chapters. But feel free to skip around based on which sections you feel are most relevant to where you are in your career right now.

Let's dive in.

DON'T CALL IT

PART ONE

Evaluate and Reevaluate

Part One should give you a clearer picture of your career and your career goals. You'll think carefully about whether quitting is really the best decision right now, and what some alternatives might be.

CHAPTER 1

GET UNSTUCK

WHO CAN BENEFIT FROM A NEW OUTLOOK ON WORK

This book is for working professionals facing a specific type of career quandary. You have a job that treats you and pays you reasonably well, though it's not quite satisfying you intellectually or creatively. In some cases, you can't realistically quit or look for something new right now. And so you feel trapped.

In other cases, you might technically have the bandwidth to look for a more exciting opportunity, but it would be more valuable if you learned how to shape your current role into something wonderful.

It doesn't matter how old you are, how seasoned you are, or where your job title falls in the corporate hierarchy. It's more about how you *feel* about your career right now. If you're feeling stuck and confused and like you could use some guidance, the insights and advice in these 12 chapters can help.

This book is not for everyone.

Most people have room to improve their work experience, regardless of their occupation, industry, or wage level. But it would be unhelpful to pretend that all workers have the same level of discretion over how they spend their time. Knowledge workers—think accountants, lawyers, and consultants—typically (though not always) have more flexibility than other types of employees around when, where, and how they get stuff done. They are the audience I'm writing for. In the future, I hope to do something similar for the rest of the working population.

I also want to be clear about why I'm writing primarily for employees versus employers. It's true that employers shape the work experience at their organizations. That said, this book is filling a gap I noticed both as a careers reporter and as a working professional who's never really managed a team. When you look at the books currently available in the business and self-improvement categories, you tend to see one of two formats. The first is geared toward people managers, telling them how to keep their teams engaged, productive, and happy. The second is geared toward individual workers, telling them how and why to quit their job and find a new one.

Books that fall outside these formats certainly exist, but they're rarer. The implication here is that the only things individual employees can do to make their jobs better are become a manager or quit.

As I progressed in my career, I would have liked a book that helped me enjoy work more—without quitting my job and without a manager title. I'm writing this book to start filling that void. After all, most people aren't managers, and most Americans don't aspire to be.[1] My hope is that this book will help you to better understand how to improve the quality of your work experience.

An important note before we move on: If you feel that you're working in a toxic environment and that quitting would be best for your mental health, you should certainly do that. The advice and strategies outlined in this book are not designed to make issues like an abusive boss or a discriminatory workplace disappear. Toward the end of this book, you'll find a resources section that includes an article to help you identify a toxic workplace and get out of it.

THE GREAT RESIGNATION

When I started writing this book, the coronavirus pandemic had been under way for a year, and it had ravaged the US labor market.

A Pew Research Center survey published in September 2020 found that 25 percent of US adults said they or someone in their household lost work because of the pandemic.[2] Leaving a stable job if you were lucky enough to have one seemed inadvisable, since there was no guarantee you'd find something else. In many cases, the wisest choice was to tough it out.

But then spring 2021 arrived. And things started to change.

Economists and career experts called it the Great Resignation, as workers across industries started quitting their jobs in droves. Kevin Roose, of the *New York Times*, dubbed it the YOLO Economy (as in, "you only live once").[3] "For a growing number of people with financial cushions and in-demand skills," Roose wrote, "the dread and anxiety of the past year are giving way to a new kind of professional fearlessness."

The past year had been tragic—millions of lives were lost around the world. At the same time, for many elite professionals who had stayed safe from the virus, the time was also something of a reset, during which they learned more about what really mattered to them. Away from the office and without their daily commute, they spent more time with family; they adopted pets; they took long walks; they baked bread and read novels. They had few if any social plans and spent little money. They had time—sometimes too much time—to think. (I started writing the proposal for this book while bunking in with my in-laws in suburban New Jersey in 2020. That was partly because I had very little else to do when the workday ended, having no children of my own to attend to.)

When vaccinations became widely available, and the job market started heating up, a large pool of working professionals felt empowered to make major life and career changes to pursue their dreams. They quit their stable jobs as bankers and pediatricians to become DJs and artists.[4]

Which left everyone else looking on longingly, wondering what the hell they were still doing at a desk, crunching numbers or writing memos or answering client emails. Sure, a new career sounded like fun. But what about their kids, who still needed diapers and snacks and soccer lessons? What about their student loans, which hung like an albatross over their financial freedom? It's not always so easy or so realistic to take a leap, even when everyone else seems to be jumping.[5]

It's also important to understand what the Great Resignation—and the overall evolution of workplace dynamics in the pandemic's wake—is really about. It's about agency: people finally getting to choose where, when, and most importantly how they work, instead of letting their employers make these decisions for them.

Consider: A Morning Consult survey conducted in May 2021 found that 39 percent of workers would quit their jobs if their employers required them to come back into the office full-time.[6] And many professionals whose employers do offer flexibility have moved to new cities, or even countries, in search of a different pace of life. Meanwhile, as of this writing, the job market is red hot, and workers in industries like tech are getting poached by companies that will pay them more to do essentially the same job they're doing now.

But that's not the whole story. While a sizable number of employees are jumping ship to new opportunities, the majority of us are staying where we are. And these individuals are who this book is for.

Now if you feel like there's another opportunity for you out there, one that will allow you to craft the life and career you really want, you should take it. My goal is to provide some guidance—and some hope—for the frustrated onlookers who feel like there isn't necessarily a better opportunity for them within reach. And to help those who are disenchanted with their work situation recognize that, with a few small changes, they could feel happier and more fulfilled by the role they have now.

In fact, because of the mass exodus of talent that's under way, workers who stay in their current organizations may find they have meaningful leverage. Many employers today are practically bending over backward to keep their employees engaged—and to keep them, period. These workers know they have influence—and their bosses know, too. Big banks like Goldman Sachs and Citi are introducing sabbatical programs and expanding their family leave benefits in an effort to keep their employees' eyes from wandering.[7]

Working from home during the pandemic awakened new work/life options for many professionals.

High performers especially may be in a better position than ever before to get what they want, whether that's the option to work from home a few days a week, take on new projects that they're more excited about, or simply receive additional feedback from their managers. These seemingly small interventions can have huge payoffs in terms of how happy and liberated you feel at work.

These are the kinds of changes that can help people like Ed, who left behind his dream job of sportscasting to take a role in PR because it offered stability and better pay. And Annafi Wahed, a whip-smart young professional who took a job at a prestigious consulting firm to bulk up her résumé and found the work impossibly draining. And Barbara, who works in her dream occupation and is among the highest performers at her firm but is nonetheless mistreated by her bosses. (We'll meet all these individuals again a little later.)

The rest of this book is fundamentally about how to navigate the decision to stay in your current job and make not just the best of it, but *more* of it.

HOW IT WOULD FEEL TO QUIT

When this book first started to take shape in my head, I called a close friend who spent several years managing talent strategy for a fast-growing tech startup. He shared with me an exercise that can help clarify things when you feel stuck at work and ready to quit.

You can start, he told me, by mentally playing out your quitting fantasy. Everyone's fantasy looks different. Yours might start with the sound of the office door slamming behind you, or the look on your boss's face when you tell her you're outta here. Someone else might envision being in her new role, running her own fashion business from her living room, without anyone to answer to.

Envisioning how you'd feel after quitting your job can help you identify what you need more of in your current role.

Take a moment to indulge that fantasy. Instead of focusing on the specific series of events, focus on the way you feel. Liberated? Energized? Empowered? Get as granular as you can here.

My friend said it's important to identify those feelings, because, chances are, they're what you really want. Quitting can certainly be a way to achieve those feelings; in fact, it could be the best way. But in his experience—and in mine—it's rarely the only way.

Exploring alternatives to quitting—even if you ultimately decide to quit—is a worthwhile exercise for (at least) two reasons. On a practical level, you might hit on a strategy that doesn't involve losing your primary source of income or going back to school and learning the skills for a new job function. From a more existential perspective, you'll also start thinking about what *you* can do to improve your work experience.

Though it might seem like you're stuck, this is in fact the ultimate move for exercising agency in your career. It doesn't matter that the labor market is soft, or that your boss is a megalomaniac. This isn't about the labor market, and this isn't about your boss. This is about you, and about the tools that you can use to feel less miserable at your day job.

These tools transcend the specific job and quandary you're in today. Whatever skills you develop now will stay with you for the rest of your career, regardless of macroeconomic factors or the particular place where you work. But today is a really good time to start trying to reshape your work experience. With workers across industries quitting en masse, those who stay may find they have considerable leverage. Many bosses are going to great lengths to keep people around.

Each chapter in this book will introduce people in a range of job functions and industries who transformed their experience of work through different means. You'll meet executives who devised simple fixes for the most tedious parts of their jobs. You'll meet startup founders who approached the transition from full-time employment to entrepreneurship cautiously and systematically. You'll also meet the social scientists and career coaches whose research lends additional credence to these varied strategies.

Many of the professionals whose stories appear in this book *did* ultimately leave their jobs. But they didn't spend every moment before they quit feeling miserable. Instead they found ways to make their work experience more palatable and accumulated skills that would help them land their next role.

Let's be clear: Thinking this way isn't easy, at least not when you're the person with the terrible job and no exit strategy. The natural impulse is often to sever ties and jump to something new. So be as patient and compassionate with yourself as you can.

And remember: Sometimes quitting *is* the best choice. I've included a chapter on how to make that transition, too. But it's worth considering whether that's the only way to achieve your personal and professional goals. Do you need to quit and start something new—or do you need to feel more power and independence than you do right now?

REMEMBER THIS

- It's always worth exploring alternatives to quitting. The process encourages you to focus on what *you* can do to improve your work experience.
- Workers who stay in their jobs when many of their colleagues are quitting may have extra leverage when asking their employers for what they want.
- Thinking about how it would feel to quit can help you figure out what you're really seeking in leaving your job.

TRY THIS

IMAGINE YOU'VE QUIT

Imagine you've done it. You've quit your job.

You've just given notice to your manager; in a few weeks you won't work here anymore.

- How do you feel? Jot down the first few emotions that come to mind.
- Who's the first person you're going to call or text with your news?
- What's the first thing you're going to do when the workday is over—have a celebratory drink? Take a long walk or run? Break down in tears of relief?

Record all these thoughts, too.

As you continue reading, these notes and images will come in handy by helping you identify what's missing in your career.

CHAPTER 2

QUITTING ISN'T THE ONLY ANSWER

PR DIRECTOR VERSUS SPORTSCASTER

Ed is the media relations director at a large university. But ever since he was a kid, when he'd watch Sunday football with his dad, his true passion has been sportscasting. Ed remembers his dad constructing a headset with Sony earphones and a wire hanger, which Ed would wear when he practiced announcing each play.

I knew Ed in his capacity as media relations director for the university; he'd helped me get in touch with a few professors for my *Insider* stories. When I emailed Ed to ask about a faculty member who might be able to help with this book, he mentioned that he happened to have a personal story in line with what I was writing about. He asked only that I use a pseudonym and obscure the details of his current and past employment. "The broadcasting industry is very small," he said, "and since I would like to get back into it one day, I would like to protect my identity."

Ed told me he adored being a broadcast journalist. He spent part of his career covering breaking news during the week and sports games on weekends, and he thrived in both environments. But Ed admittedly finds little thrill in his current role heading up media relations for the university.

"What's missing," he told me, "is the excitement of doing live television, the thrill of working in a fast-paced environment, and the camaraderie that I felt in the newsroom." He said it's virtually impossible to replicate "the satisfaction of putting a product on the air and having it look good after rushing around like crazy for hours to make it possible." The media relations job is somewhat creatively stifling, since it mostly involves writing and pitching press releases about one scientific study after another. "The thrill of getting a story in the *Washington Post* isn't quite the same as it was in my first year on the job," he said.

I asked Ed what was stopping him from getting back into journalism, and specifically sports announcing. Money, he told me. Ed and his ex-partner, a high school teacher, rent a townhouse (and own a pet rabbit); Ed is still paying down his student loans. Most significantly, Ed is single-handedly supporting his mother, who stopped working her retail job during the pandemic because she was afraid of getting sick. If Ed were to leave the university and find another job in journalism, he'd be taking a pay cut—and would no longer be able to support his current lifestyle.

Time is a factor, too. If Ed were serious about applying for sportscasting jobs, he'd have to rewatch his old tapes, each one of which is about 3½ hours (the length of a standard football game).

Then there's the sheer mental energy it would take to do a complete career reset. Ed said he doesn't have that kind of energy anymore. Looking back on his twenties, when he'd park at highway rest areas for a nap in between gigs, Ed said, "Where did that drive go?"

Not to mention, his current gig is pretty cushy. At 37 years old, Ed makes upward of $100,000 and has stellar benefits. If, once in a while, he wants to take a day off work, he emails HR that morning. Ed's bosses love him, and are consistently impressed with both his creativity and his attention to detail, which is why he's received several merit raises since starting there.

But every night after dinner, Ed cracks a beer, turns on the TV, sits on the couch, and stares into space for a while. Sometimes he has no idea what he's thinking about. Most of the time, though, he's thinking about being at a game. Nothing made Ed happier than that.

Ed wouldn't give up his fantasizing about getting back into sports announcing. Maybe it's a form of self-delusion, but it's what keeps him going. On days when he's feeling dismal about his job or career, he consoles himself with the idea that maybe someday he'll be able to make a change. Still, Ed keeps these thoughts mostly to himself. "I would assume most of my colleagues believe I made the transition [to PR] and I'm happy where I am," he said. "I don't think I've shared with anyone that I still actively ponder getting back into the business."

Then a football game comes on TV, and Ed is transported right back to his sportscasting days. "Gee," he thinks to himself, "I'd love to do that again."

NAME THE OBSTACLES BETWEEN YOU AND QUITTING

The process of reshaping your job starts with a step you can do anywhere, anytime: Think about all the very good reasons *not* to quit right now. These might be external factors, like the fact that your desired industry doesn't have a lot of openings; or your reasons might be more personal, like the fact that this job will look great on your résumé and will open doors for you down the road. This exercise might sound simple, and that's because it is.

For example, you might say to yourself, "I'm here because this job will make me a stronger candidate for a career in politics, which is where I really want to work." Ed might say something like, "I'm staying in this job so that I can support my mom and the lifestyle I want."

When you say these things out loud (or in your own head), it can be easier to see the rationale behind staying at your job for now. This mindset shift can be powerful, because it reminds you that you are ultimately in control of your career. You could, in theory, leave your unfulfilling job today. But that decision wouldn't necessarily jibe with the life you want, or the life you're trying to build.

Reminding yourself of why you stay in your current job can help you to see your situation more objectively and to make better career decisions.

There are myriad motivations for sticking with a job you don't love, but a few common reasons stand out. Many of them have to do with money.

Take student debt. In the United States, the cost of college has soared over the past few decades, to the point where many would-be students are questioning its value.[1] As of November 2021, 45 million people in the United States owe a total of $1.75 trillion in student loans.[2]

And research suggests that student debt shapes graduates' subsequent career choices. One 2011 study found that graduates with student debt choose higher-paying jobs (think banking or consulting) and are less likely to pursue lower-paying, public interest jobs (think legal aid attorney or public school teacher) than their peers without debt.[3] And a 2017 working paper found that graduates with debt are less picky about job offers in the near term because it's more pressing that they find *something* that will allow them to pay their monthly student loan bills.[4]

The career costs of caregiving, meanwhile, can be steep. The US Department of Agriculture reports that middle-income, married-couple parents of a child born in 2015 will spend about $233,610 for food, housing, and other necessities before their kid turns 17.[5] That *doesn't* include the cost of college.

There are also less tangible—but equally valid—reasons for staying at a job, like getting to tell prospective employers that you worked at Google, or Goldman Sachs, or someplace equally prestigious.

Or you might not have the stomach for quitting without something else perfectly lined up. After all, certain professionals are more risk averse than others. Some workers can tolerate the seeming tedium of their job if it provides some stability, whereas others in their position would go stir-crazy. People are different. The critical thing is to know yourself and what you care about.

This kind of introspection can be challenging. It's easier to think about who we'd *like* to be (a bold and daring entrepreneur) or who we think we *should* be (someone whose job involves giving back to the community) than it is to recognize who we are today. But when you stop constantly comparing yourself with these alternate personas, you may find it frees up some mental energy.

Two critical components of self-awareness that psychologists have identified are aspirations and fit. According to organizational psychologist Tasha Eurich, "aspirations" refer to what you want to experience and achieve in life, and "fit" describes the environment you need to feel happy and engaged.[6] If you're not sure what your aspirations are or what kind of work environment you fit (and thrive) in, it's that much harder to build a satisfying career.

The important thing to remember is that no matter what your specific reasons for staying are, you're not alone. There are a lot of people who, for whatever reason, feel tethered to jobs they don't love. And it's not always that they're afraid of taking a risk or flouting social expectations, as so many inspirational posters would have it. Beyond fear, there are very real, legitimate, and common reasons for staying at an imperfect job.

As for the Great Resignation, it may be but a blip in a broader trend in which job tenure—how long people spend with a single employer—is actually increasing. For all the media coverage of millennial and Generation Z job-hoppers, economists say people are switching employers *less often* than they did in the 1980s.[7]

Economists can't say for sure whether lengthening job tenures overall is a good thing. It could be, the Federal Reserve Bank of Minneapolis economist Abigail Wozniak told me, that many people feel stuck, like they don't have a better option than where they are now. It could also be that people are finding a fit sooner than they used to, and so they don't feel a pressing need to switch. More research is needed to identify workers' motivations for sticking with their employer. The point is that you aren't the only person who's been at your company for 5, 10, or 15 years, even if it feels that way.

Now, practical motivations for staying aren't always fun to talk about, especially compared to your friend's thriller about telling her old boss to shove it and starting her now-thriving fashion business the very next morning. Let's spend a little time exploring the reasons why certain career stories seem more compelling than others—and why falling for these fairy tale–esque narratives can be dangerous.

TELL A DIFFERENT CAREER STORY

At *Insider*, my colleagues and I have published plenty of stories about folks who "gave it all up." Think: She was a lawyer making six figures, and now she's an entrepreneur running a YouTube advice channel;[8] she was a high-flying consultant, and now she's a business coach and TikTok influencer.[9]

These stories are inherently compelling, and that's likely because they have a clear narrative arc. Here's a hypothetical example:

Sara was working in marketing; she didn't feel creatively fulfilled; one day she told her boss she was quitting; now she makes and sells her own jewelry, and she's never felt freer or happier.

The story starts with a simple problem: Sara doesn't like her job. Then there's the climax: Sara triumphantly announces her resignation. Finally, we have the resolution: Sara frees herself from the shackles of corporate life and starts a business she's passionate about. The End.

Now here's a hypothetical example of the story you'd tell about someone who didn't jump to something new:

Sara was working in marketing; she didn't feel creatively fulfilled, but her family relied on the top-notch benefits; she found a way to make every workday a little brighter, and she's still at the same company today.

The story starts with the same problem: Sara doesn't like her job. But now we've got a complicating factor: Sara has a family, and she's able to sustain said family with the healthcare benefits her employer provides.

In this story, there's no triumphant climax. Maybe Sara asks her boss for more of the kind of projects she enjoys, or maybe she reframes her work experience to think about all the clients she helps on a daily basis. Now the workday's a little easier to get through, and Sara likes her job a little more. The . . . End?

We're drawn to stories that make sense, that have simultaneously a sense of closure and possibility. That second Sara story seems like it doesn't fit the bill, but it's certainly more realistic. I'd also argue that the second story is just as powerful as the first. Imagine how much agency that second Sara must have if she turned her deadening experience into something more palatable, or even enjoyable, while still caring for her family.

To understand why certain types of career stories are inherently more appealing than others, it helps to know a little about the field of narrative identity.

Narrative Identity and Career Stories

To help make sense of our life experiences, we craft stories around them. The same is true for our career trajectory. We try to piece together job interviews, promotions, hirings, and firings into a perfectly coherent narrative, the kind you could tell little kids so that they'd understand.

Research suggests there's one type of life story that appeals especially strongly to American adults. It's called a "redemptive narrative," and what happens is the narrator triumphs over or is freed by some kind of adversity.[10] Or the narrator goes through adversity only to have something positive come out of it.

In a career context, maybe you lost one job and subsequently found another. The redemptive narrative you tell might involve learning that the first job wasn't right for you anyway, so it's a good thing you ended up losing it and finding something better. The event sequence now makes sense and has meaning, instead of looking like a series of relatively arbitrary happenings.

But the cultural demand for redemptive narratives can be troublesome. Jonathan Adler, a professor of psychology at Olin College of Engineering, co-runs the Health Story Collaborative in Cambridge, Massachusetts, where he helps patients with serious illnesses cope with their diagnoses through storytelling. Many of these individuals, Adler said, feel a "press for redemption," like something great is supposed to come out of their experience of illness.

But "for a lot of people," Adler said, their diagnoses "just suck." There's no redemption to be found. And now the problem is twofold. "You have an illness narrative, which is not a narrative people love to hear," Adler said. And "it isn't a redemptive story. It hasn't shown you something good about yourself. So people feel doubly cursed by this experience."

People can feel a similar kind of undue pressure to turn their careers into redemptive narratives. If your boss is mean and your clients are wretched, maybe you want to tell your friends over drinks that "Hey, at least this experience is teaching me how to deal with assholes!" when, really, it just feels torturous on a daily basis. In a way, it would be easier to cope with your unsavory boss and clients if you could just admit how terrible they are.

How to Respond When Someone Tells You a Career Story Without a Happy Ending

The way we respond to other people's stories about their lives and careers can make a difference in how they feel about those experiences. When you're listening to friends or colleagues recount something distressing that happened in their professional life—maybe they were unexpectedly fired or maybe they got passed over for a promotion they'd earned—see if you can resist the impulse to press them to see the so-called silver lining.

In general, Americans (including many psychotherapists[11]) like a story with a happy ending, but that inclination can easily alienate people who don't feel that their story ends so neatly or satisfyingly. Research led by Kate McLean, a professor of psychology at Western Washington University, found that people in the United States preferred traumatic stories that were redemptive over similar stories that ended on a negative note.[12] They also perceived the people who told these traumatic-turned-redemptive narratives as healthier than people who told other types of stories.

But as McLean and her colleagues observed, "Someone who does not redeem trauma may be unheard, devalued, or isolated." Someone who does not redeem trauma may also, the researchers wrote, avoid telling a fully authentic life story, which in turn means that it's harder for people to really get to know that person.

So try not to remind your friends or colleagues that now they can find a job they really love, or that they probably wouldn't have liked the extra job responsibilities that came with the promotion anyway. Instead see if you can hold space for their disappointment and frustration—for whatever they're feeling—and let them craft the kind of career story that makes sense to them. That way, they won't feel additionally burdened by the pressure to assure you that everything's great.

The Promise and Peril of Agency

Like redemption, agency can be a double-edged sword in life stories, too. Sometimes it's good for us: One study Adler published found that psychotherapy patients experienced improved mental health after they started writing about their life experiences as though they had greater agency over their experiences.[13] As the author wrote in the 2012 paper, "Individuals begin to tell new stories and then live their way into them."

But feeling *too* much agency over your life and career can backfire. McLean told me she suspects most people in the United States have been taught, or subtly influenced by family, friends, educators, and the media, to think that they can more or less determine the course of their lives and careers.

Changing your life by changing your story can be harder than it seems. Sometimes there are barriers between you and your ideal life or career.

"What we *don't* understand," McLean said, "are the limits to change." Telling off your boss, leaving your job, and starting a jewelry business from scratch are hard to do. Really hard. If you do it right, it takes careful planning, and even then everything might not work out. In some cases, people who follow this path might even grieve their old work lives, routines, and compatriots.

"There's this idea that you can change your life by changing your story," McLean said. What that mantra doesn't take into account, she added, is the barriers that might exist between you and the ideal life or career narrative. Sometimes these barriers are external and largely out of your control, like if you lost your job but there's a recession and it's hard to find another job. Even barriers that are more specific to the individual can be legitimately difficult to overcome. In second Sara's case, her family relies on the benefits that her employer provides. Maybe she even likes some aspects of the work and worries about straying from the devil she knows, so to speak.

I asked Adler how to reconcile all these ideas about life narratives, and he mentioned that just being aware of the pressure to craft a redemptive career narrative can be helpful. It won't turn a bad job into an incredible one. But it will relieve some of the pressure you might be feeling to pretend everything's OK.

I also prodded Adler to tell me whether we should believe that we're steering the course of our career trajectory. He suggested, wisely, that agency doesn't always have to take such an obvious form, like slamming the office door in your boss's face or moving across the country to start a company from scratch. Sometimes, he said, it's more about shifting your perspective.

"The only option is not *change the objective reality*," Adler said. "You can change your *outlook* on the objective reality, and that can be really helpful." To use his example, maybe your boss doesn't recognize your unique skills and talents, but you can console yourself with the knowledge that your friends and family do.

That approach made sense to me. You can believe you're in control of your career, but you can also believe that there's more than one way to steer. Quitting and starting something new is certainly a possibility. So is changing your outlook so that you're less peeved by your boss's slights. So is spending more time with colleagues you like, connecting the work back to your personal values, or even getting a hobby outside of work. (These are all strategies we'll explore in Part Two.)

To stick with the literary metaphors, you get to narrate your story *and* choose the genre. Again, we're not looking for perfection here. What we want is some distance between a demoralizing work experience you've gone through and how you feel about yourself overall.

And there are so many second Saras out there, understandably concerned about overhauling their lives and careers, that it's worth letting people know there are other options besides fairy tales.

We can all be like second Sara, who stayed at the marketing job she didn't love. It just takes some willingness to let go of the narratives about success and happiness that we've held onto for so long. Reshaping our work experience often means holding those career stories up to the light until we can see where they're starting to come apart.

With that in mind, let's get back to Ed's story.

THE PR DIRECTOR'S REDEMPTION

We can think about Ed's career dilemma in the context of redemptive narratives and agency. By any objective standards, Ed is doing pretty well. He makes a six-figure salary that allows him to rent a comfortable house and support his mom; he has a job that draws at least somewhat on his creativity and his passion for storytelling; he's climbed the proverbial ladder by impressing his bosses. But he doesn't feel entirely satisfied with the career path he's on.

In a redemptive narrative, the kind that might play out in a fairy tale or a romantic comedy, Ed would wake up one day and decide he's sick of everything and he's giving it all up to pursue his longtime dream of becoming a famous sportscaster. For a while, Ed's mom would be upset. For a while, he'd have no money coming in. But then Ed would get his big break—his redemption—and everyone would cheer him on as he finally turned his career fantasies into reality and lived a life of passion and fulfillment. It would be a double win: Ed would get a job in sportscasting, and he would feel proud of himself for demonstrating agency by making that change happen.

I'm not ruling out the possibility that this obvious kind of redemption might happen for Ed someday. Yet I also want Ed, and every professional in a similar position, to know that he's not a failure if this *doesn't* happen. If Ed and the others don't get the job they really want, they can still feel proud of themselves for what they've achieved in their career. They can still feel happy.

When I prompted Ed to think about ways in which he could shift either his mindset or his actual work responsibilities, he sighed. "I think it all comes back to something I'm really, really bad at," he said. "And that is not taking it personally."

Ed could, theoretically, try to see his current job as just a job. Maybe he could pick up a hobby—related to sports announcing or not—that draws more heavily on his skills and passions. Maybe that would help him see his media relations work as an activity that pays the bills even if it doesn't fulfill him on a personal level.

"But I invest so much of myself into each thing, whatever that might be," Ed told me. "It's not in my DNA to just do a good-enough job. I always want it to be as perfect as it can possibly be." When he writes a press release or a pitch, "I feel like it's got to be perfect or I'm letting myself down and I'm letting the people involved down." It's as if he's constantly putting his all into something that doesn't love him in return.

There are, unfortunately, no easy solutions here. After all, Ed's personality and his orientation to work aren't going to magically change. Perhaps the best approach is for Ed to give a little more weight to what's going well and, moreover, to what he's *doing* well in his career. Ed's ability to craft stories out of new academic research is impeccable. He's good with deadlines; he always follows through. And again, he has singlehandedly parlayed his journalism experience into something lucrative enough that he can support his family. To me, Ed is a really impressive person and professional. It's a matter of getting him to see himself the same way.

Common Reasons People Don't Quit

A 2018 survey from HR consulting firm Randstad highlights some common reasons why US workers stay in jobs they don't love.[14] Here are some of the most intriguing findings:

- Seventy-eight percent stay to keep their benefits package.
- Seventy-one percent stay because it's easier than starting something new.
- Fifty-six percent stay because taking a new job might mean having less paid time off at first.
- Fifty-four percent stay because they're the primary financial providers for their families.

REMEMBER THIS

- Job tenures in the United States have increased since the 1980s, research shows. Which means you aren't the only person who's been with your employer for a while.
- There are many legitimate reasons for sticking with a job you don't love. Sometimes it helps to remind yourself exactly why you're staying at your job for now.
- Taking control of your career is broader than just slamming the door in your boss's face and leaving to start something of your own. Reclaiming agency can be as simple as shifting your perspective on your boss's slights.

TRY THIS

ARTICULATE WHY YOU'RE STILL HERE

First, identify two of the most pressing motivations for staying at your job right now.

Next, write two sentences about those motivations that explain why staying at your job aligns with your values: For example, "I'm here because this job pays me a lot, which allows me to send my kids to schools that fit their educational needs." Or "I'm here because my employer is flexible and I can take about as much vacation time as I want, which allows me to pursue my favorite hobby: travel."

Crafting these statements is unlikely to immediately make you feel better about your job situation. But it will remind you that you've made the decision to stay and that staying fits with the life you're trying to build.

CHAPTER 3

WHAT'S THE REAL PROBLEM?

YOU CAN'T RUN FROM YOUR DEMONS

It's tempting to believe that cutting and running—throwing your hands up, if you will—will solve all your problems. You can see evidence of that inclination in the explosion of career coaching during the pandemic.[1] People are looking for guidance as they try to locate their next home on a map of all the possible professional paths they could pursue.

But the answer to your discontent, whether with work or with life overall, isn't always to jump to something newer and shinier. The same problems that existed in your original job may sneak up on you in the next one, suggesting that perhaps the problem lies in the type of roles you're drawn to.

Rebecca Fraser-Thill, a Portland, Maine–based career coach who was until recently an instructor in Bates College's psychology department and Center for Purposeful Work, told me in spring 2021 that she'd never seen greater demand for her services. Many of her clients and prospective clients had realized during the pandemic that what they thought was important to them—a fancy job title, a hefty salary—wasn't really. Now, Fraser-Thill said, "they want to reorder their lives around 'What does it look like to feel fulfilled and impactful in my day-to-day?'"

Fraser-Thill always applauds the move to find what fulfills and energizes you. She loves when her clients can feel the positive impact they're making on others. (I know this firsthand: Fraser-Thill was my coach back in 2017, and I wrote a story about my experience working with her.[2]) But as the waitlist for her coaching programs grew ever longer that spring, she became somewhat concerned.

"I actually worry that some of this won't stick with people," she told me. "When you take too big of a leap from an emotional place," she said, especially without doing the necessary research and experimentation to make sure this is what you really want, "it tends to not stick for the long haul." In fact, Fraser-Thill is already seeing some new clients who made a huge career pivot thinking it would fix everything, but they still feel unfulfilled.

That observation lines up with what other trendspotters are seeing.[3] In fall 2021, my *Insider* colleague Aki Ito published an article forecasting the influx of "boomerang employees," specifically folks who quit their jobs in the Great Resignation to pursue something else and now want their old gigs back.[4]

Yet even before the Great Resignation began, Fraser-Thill wanted to help her clients avoid costly career mistakes. Fraser-Thill works primarily with high-achieving professionals who are looking for something more out of their careers. Typically, they want greater happiness and fulfillment—a role that will really capitalize on their unique skills and passions. Most of them assume that getting there will require some kind of major pivot, or at least a new job at a new organization. So they seek Fraser-Thill's guidance on launching this transition process.

Fraser-Thill never rules out the possibility of a career change. But she also makes a point of gently challenging her clients' assumptions about where they'll find the kind of happiness and fulfillment they're seeking. She's big on pushing her clients to see the motivation, or the "why," behind the things they want. She also helps them pinpoint exactly what they don't like about their work experience.

It sounds obvious: Figure out what the problem is before you start trying to solve it. But when you're feeling stuck in your job, and miserable every weekday morning, it's easy to assume that everything stinks—and will never get better. This is rarely true.

"We tend to jump in," Fraser-Thill told me. *Frustrated at work? Quit that job and get a new one!* "And that's exactly the block for a lot of people for meaningful work," she added. We're too quick to look for solutions, skipping over that critical introspection around what the issue really is.

Maybe the problem is that you feel undervalued or overworked or that your skills and talents aren't being utilized. Maybe you and your boss have different communication styles; maybe your desk mate brags too much and makes you feel bad.

You're more likely to achieve happiness and fulfillment at work when you identify what you like and dislike about your job.

When you frame the situation this way, it's easier to see that the thing you're looking for isn't necessarily a new job or a new company. The thing you're looking for is more appreciation, or less work, or projects that tap into your unique abilities. Sure, maybe a new job would help you get there. But it's almost assuredly not the only way to get there. In some cases, it might even be the wrong way to get there.

Instead of big leaps, Fraser-Thill is a proponent of small shifts in the direction you think you'd like to go. For example, if you think you'd like to transition from full-time to freelance graphic design, can you take on some consulting projects first and see how they go? That way, if you stumble, or if you realize this isn't what you want to do, you can quickly reverse course and try something else. Building success incrementally is a good idea generally, since bite-sized tasks can be less overwhelming than an entire project laid out before you. But it's an especially practical idea if you're not in a position—financially or otherwise—to upend your life and face the possibility that it won't work out.

HOW I SHOULD HAVE HANDLED MY OWN JOB DISSATISFACTION

In the Preface to this book, I described a time several years ago when I felt so frustrated at work that I considered quitting. To recap: My managers kept assigning me slideshows on topics like signs that you're likable or that your relationship is on shaky footing. They weren't always my favorite stories to write, and our audience was seemingly losing interest in some of them. Instead of having an honest conversation about the issue with my editor, I started looking for other jobs. Fortunately, the search didn't pan out.

Now, hindsight is often 20/20, and it's easy for me to say now how I could or should have handled this dilemma. But I'm hopeful that the retrospective rewrite in the following pages will help any reader who's stuck in a similar situation. Here's what I might have done differently.

Step 1. I Could Have Gauged the Culture on the Team

This means asking yourself, "Do I have the kind of manager who would be receptive and even supportive if I told her I didn't like some of the work I was doing?" For some people, the answer might be absolutely not, in which case complete candor might not be the best approach. (Better to focus exclusively on the measurable outcomes these tasks are or aren't driving.) But in my case, the answer was yes, meaning there was something other than the fear of upsetting her that was behind my reluctance to be straightforward.

To be quite frank, I'm still trying to figure out what those psychological or emotional obstacles were. I suspect that, on some level, I feared the editorial powers that be wouldn't think I was skilled enough to start writing more of those feature stories. Or that I'd get the green light to start writing them and they'd turn out to be really boring. It was arguably easier to just complain about not having the support and encouragement I needed to write these pieces.

Step 2. I Could Have Explained How Doing Things Differently Would Benefit the Organization

Another thing I did reasonably well, but could have done better: framing my resistance to "signs" slideshows and my desire to do something else. In the email response to my editor, I said that these stories weren't performing so well with readers. But I could easily have gone a few steps further.

Perhaps I could have dug up statistics on slideshows that had flopped and compared them with the stats for other articles that readers had gobbled up, then figured out what made them different. Perhaps I could have pitched an alternative story idea for every slideshow I published that would have gone deeper into the very same topic. The point is this: When you're talking to your boss about dropping some of your job responsibilities, you'll want to be as specific about why and as proactive as possible about *what else we can do.*

It's a way to show you've taken ownership of your role—something many execs have told me they love to see in their employees. Not to mention that when you come prepared with data and ideas, your manager will have what's needed to approach *their* manager and make the case for you to shift your projects.

Step 3. I Shouldn't Have Assumed My Boss Knew How I Felt

Most importantly, I could have realized that my editor, however savvy and sympathetic she was, was not a mind reader. If I didn't tell her how I felt about certain assignments, there was virtually no way for her to intuit this information.

Step 4. I Should Have Given Myself Options

As for looking elsewhere, there's nothing inherently wrong with scouting out new opportunities and seeing how they compare with your current role. Netflix, in fact, encourages employees to interview for jobs outside the company and then talk about what they learn with their boss.[5]

As Patty McCord, the company's original HR chief, once told me in an interview for *Insider*, "My experience is that you're more honest with a perfect stranger than you are with your own manager after a while."[6] In other words, talking to someone who isn't your direct manager at a job you dislike can help you gain some clarity around the kind of work you'd prefer.

But moving elsewhere shouldn't have been the *only* option I was banking on. Other options included talking to my editor about my observations and ideas and seeing if, together, we could reshape my role. In fact, there's a chance that if I did get one of those other jobs I'd applied for, I might have found myself in the same predicament of getting assignments I didn't like and still being hesitant to say anything about it. Which is to say that even if ultimately you do leave your current job, the process of identifying what's valuable and what you enjoy can help you target your search for your next opportunity.

15 REVEALING QUESTIONS TO ASK YOURSELF

Before making any changes to your work experience, it helps to gain some clarity around what's going well and what's not. A coach, or even an especially thoughtful friend, can assist in this process.

You can also lead the introspection process yourself, using the following 15 questions as a guide. I encourage you to answer all of them, either in your head or on paper, though I suspect you'll benefit even if you can get to only a few. You'll see that these prompts are pretty straightforward. You may also find that you've never given them much thought—so be open to surprises.

1. What Are Your Favorite Parts of Your Current Workday?

It's easy to feel like your job is generally horrible or generally wrong for you. And while this is certainly a possibility, it's much more likely that there are some redeeming aspects of the work. Think back on how you spent the last workweek: Were there *any* times when you felt more engaged or motivated than usual? There are no wrong answers here. Even a fleeting half hour counts, and no one will fault you if the source of happiness was checking your inbox for new emails.

It's critical to identify these less-loathsome parts of your work experience and how exactly they made you feel. For example, maybe chatting with a longtime client on the phone brought you some joy yesterday. If you stay in your current role for a while, you can work on finding ways to make certain client interactions a bigger part of your workday. Even as you start plotting your next career move, knowing what you value in a job will help you target your search (and avoid winding up in a similarly frustrating situation in your next role).

Christine Cruzvergara, the chief education strategy officer at the early career network Handshake, told me how identifying what made her happy at work helped her refine a job search earlier in her career. Cruzvergara had recently finished graduate school, and she found herself antsy to move onto something else. At night, she'd browse job listings for opportunities that appealed to her and that seemed like a step up from her current gig. But it wasn't immediately clear which roles she should go after and which would be too similar to her current job.

Cruzvergara started jotting down some notes every day about when she felt most energized and when time seemed to fly by. And she learned that working with other ambitious, creative colleagues was easily the most important aspect of her work.

"People matter so much to me," she said. As for her job title and salary and how prestigious the role was, those things mattered. (Cruzvergara had bills to pay, after all.) But those factors "mattered less than I initially thought they did," she said. As long as she could support herself, it wasn't like she needed to impress people with a fancy business card.

The implications of that realization were twofold. During the day, Cruzvergara spent more time cultivating relationships with her most inspiring colleagues. That way she could enjoy her existing job more. And when she scouted out new job opportunities, Cruzvergara looked specifically for work environments that appeared to have strong team cultures where people supported each other's efforts. Eventually, she ended up with a job on the career development team at George Mason University.

2. When During Your Career Have You Felt Most Engaged?

I'm using the word "career" here, but any work or academic experience counts. Try to recall the details: what you were doing, where you were, who else was there.

This is an exercise that the career coach Rebecca Fraser-Thill uses often with her clients. Especially, she told me, with high achievers who are accustomed to looking outward for signposts of success, like promotions, raises, and praise from management. Fraser-Thill helps these individuals shift their focus by asking them, "When in the past did you think, 'I feel really good about this?'" She encourages them to think small. For example, the great feeling a client had tutoring classmates in college.

Don't get too literal—just because you enjoyed tutoring in college doesn't mean you should pivot from consulting to teaching. Instead you'll want to drill down until you can say (or at least guess) what about that experience was so gratifying. Even better if you can remember a few instances and try to find the common threads between them.

3. What Might That Gratifying Experience Look like Now?

Let's stick with the example about tutoring college classmates. Say you realize that you get a thrill out of seeing people's faces light up when they make progress on a tough challenge. If you were one of Fraser-Thill's clients, she'd ask you how you might replicate that experience or elicit that thrill today in your current role. Again, avoiding taking this too literally, you can choose to sign up as a tutor at your local library, but that's probably not the only answer here.

Avoid self-editing, too. Be as creative as possible when you brainstorm ways to achieve that feeling of making a tangible difference again. Maybe you jot down a few possibilities, including spending more time working on-site with clients and rolling up your sleeves to help them solve their trickiest problems. Or volunteering to present on an area of expertise that you have, but people on your team might not have. There are many different paths to the same emotional outcome. And sometimes just knowing that you have those options can help you feel a little lighter, even before you execute on any of them.

4. What Are the Three Most Important Attributes You Bring to a Work Environment?

These attributes can be anything from a positive, can-do attitude to the ability to focus your attention on a particular project for hours at a time. And being able to articulate your most important professional skills can help you find or create a work environment where you'll thrive. Research suggests we're most engaged at work when we're capitalizing on our unique strengths.[7]

This is how Kerri Twigg, a career coach in Manitoba, Canada, and the author of the 2021 book *The Career Stories Method*, approaches her work with clients. Twigg often draws on her background in theater arts to help her clients craft fulfilling careers. Part of her process involves having clients choose the three skills and/or passions that have shaped their work experience. Twigg's, for example, are "helping others, building programs, solving problems."[8]

One of the most powerful exercises she does during group workshops involves asking the participants to choose their three skills, then leave the room. When they come back, she instructs them to *move* around the space like a person who has those skills. At first, Twigg told me, participants will be "kind of slumped" in their seats. But when they come back embodying the three skills, their whole body language becomes more confident.

Outside the workshop room, this exercise can have powerful implications for your work experience. First, simply knowing that you're someone who brings something special to your work environment (that you're someone with a "unique value proposition," to use business lingo) can help you build confidence. And instead of feeling demoralized because this job is completely detached from what you care about and enjoy, you can train your attention on whatever aspects of the job you do feel connected to and/or uniquely skilled at. The important thing to remember is that you need to be able to articulate your skills and passions before you can begin to appreciate the parts of your job that draw on those things.

5. What's Most Important to You in a Job Right Now?

You're allowed and even encouraged to come up with more than one answer here. For example, you can say, "career development opportunities" and "making a positive impact on the world around me." But make sure you're being honest with yourself. (Shame is not part of this questions exercise.) If pay and prestige top the list, be sure to acknowledge that.

In Christine Cruzvergara's experience, "If you end up taking a job that doesn't meet some of the needs that you have, you're going to end up being really dissatisfied and you're going to feel less engaged." That's true whether you place the most value on relationships with colleagues or on a big paycheck. Keep in mind, too, that your values will likely evolve over time. A certain amount of introspection will always be necessary.

6. Is It Conceivable That You Might Get Those Things from Your Current Role?

Things get a little tricky here. If money is most important to you right now and your job pays a magnitude less than you need to live the lifestyle you want, it's likely that you'll have to do some extra training to transition onto a more lucrative career path.

But if you're a corporate lawyer or a consultant and you value making a positive difference in the world, don't assume you're out of luck (as so many of my lawyer and consultant friends tend to do).

Does it seem at all plausible that if you shifted your outlook—maybe taking a beat to appreciate how delighted your clients are when you help them—or shifted some of your daily job responsibilities—maybe adding some pro bono work—you might feel like you're making that difference?

7. Do You Remember What Drew You to This Job in the First Place?

Years ago, I interviewed the University of Pennsylvania psychologist and *Grit* author Angela Duckworth for an *Insider* video series.[9] ("Grit," according to Duckworth, is a combination of passion and perseverance that strongly predicts success in life.) I asked Duckworth for her thoughts on when quitting a job is appropriate and when it's simply "ungritty." She recommended asking yourself: "What am I here for? What is it about this job that first attracted me?"

So try to remember some of the reasons you took this job—maybe it was out of desperation, but maybe the challenging work tasks appealed to you, or maybe your prospective colleagues seemed inspiring. (If you took any notes during the interview or made a list of pros and cons after getting an offer, this would be a good time to dig them up.) It can be easy to lose sight of these attributes once you're in the weeds.

8. What's the Gap Between What You Expected This Job to Be like When You Started and What It's like Now?

It's possible the company simply put on its best face during the interview process, leaving the unsavory aspects of its work culture undisclosed. It's also possible that *your* personal values and interests have changed over time so that what was once important to you in a job is less so now.

You can examine the delta between your expectations and current reality as a way of figuring out whether quitting is advisable. In the *Insider* interview, Duckworth said that if you can answer the question above (about what first drew you to this company) with, "Well, this is what first attracted me in this direction, but actually this other company would be a better way for me to meet that goal," then you may very well want to make a move when it's feasible.

But if what attracted you then still appeals to you now, it may help to reconnect with the broader mission of your team or organization. In his 2019 book, *How to Win*, the *New York Times* journalist Neil Irwin explains how big-picture thinkers are typically the most successful in their careers.[10] These people understand where their industry is headed and how their company fits into that, and even more importantly, what their organization's purpose is and how their job fits into that.[11]

One of the most concrete ways to get a sense of these things is to ask your manager about their top priorities for the next quarter as well as upper management's goals. Think about how your daily tasks are helping management meet those goals and fulfill the organization's overall purpose.

9. What Are Your Least Favorite Parts of Your Workday?

Answering this question is important, because while it's likely that you spend a lot of time thinking about how terrible your job is, it's possible that you don't know *exactly* what's making you miserable. So be specific about the tasks and interactions that drain you or feel creatively stifling. For example, "managing the editorial calendar for my team" is a more helpful response in this case than "administrative work."

Don't discount the small stuff, either. Some of the most enlightening research I've covered for *Insider* shows how much people underestimate the pain of commuting.[12] Based on this research, it's likely that if you moved within walking distance of your office or biked instead of drove to the office (assuming you're working from an office right now), you'd feel significantly happier during the workday.

There are plenty of other seemingly trivial items that end up being barriers to our job satisfaction. Think having overflowing inboxes, sitting too close to the trash can, or being stuck with a very un-ergonomic desk chair. Before you start tackling the big stuff (like that editorial calendar management), see if any of these small tweaks will make a difference.

10. How Do Your Least Favorite Parts of Your Workday Make You Feel?

We're going one step further in our introspection here. So you hate managing the editorial calendar for your team. Can you come up with a few words to describe how you *feel* when you're doing that task? (Anxious, harried, resentful, frustrated, confused, bored—these are all options.)

This exercise is something like the reverse of Fraser-Thill's exercise (from Questions 2 and 3), in which you think about the best points in your career and how they made you feel. Fraser-Thill's exercise is helpful because it gets you thinking about other ways to achieve that feeling, or that level of engagement, again.

In this case, articulating how you feel while doing your least favorite tasks can help you think about ways you might change those tasks so they aren't associated with so much angst. To stick with the editorial calendar example, are you frustrated and bored because you feel this task is below your pay grade? If so, perhaps you can train someone junior to take on this responsibility, or perhaps you can look into automating some of the processes so you can spend time on more creative pursuits.

11. Why Do You Think Your Managers Have You Perform These Tasks?

Another way to frame this question is, "What outcomes are these loathsome tasks driving?" It goes back to big-picture thinking (from Question 8). Sometimes your tasks can seem a little more tolerable if you understand how they fit into the organization's overall mission. At least you'll feel like you're helping move the business ahead, instead of typing into a void.

It's also possible that you'll give this question some thought and realize the tasks *aren't* driving many substantive results. This is similar to what happened to me earlier in my career, when I learned that certain types of slideshows were no longer grabbing readers' attention. This is a pretty good reason to ask to stop doing these tasks; the important thing is how you frame that request to your manager. If you come armed with data on the lack of results associated with these tasks *and* if you present some ideas for other projects that would drive positive outcomes, your manager will have a hard time turning you down.

12. If You Told Your Manager Today How You Wanted to Reshape Your Role, How Do You Think Your Manager Would React?

When you're thinking about shaping your work experience, it's important to know whether and how much to involve your boss. There are plenty of ways to improve your workday *without* your boss's permission or even knowledge—we'll address those in the chapter on job crafting.

But if you have a manager who's any combination of understanding, flexible, and excited about new ideas, you may very well want to get your manager on board.

So imagine that you sat down (or got on a phone call) with your boss and explained some of the tasks you'd like to do more of and some of the tasks you'd like to do less of. Imagine that you made a solid case for these changes based on how they'd help the team and the company. What do you think your manager would say? If you envision a hesitant reaction, what do you imagine it would take to convince your manager?

You can also consider the feelings that your manager's likely reaction will elicit in you. Do you imagine feeling ashamed and defeated? Inspired to keep forging ahead? If you can predict how you might feel in that moment, you can start thinking about ways to make the conversation with your boss less stressful for you.

13. If You're Not That Concerned About Your Manager's Reaction, What Else Might Be Stopping You from Making Some Changes at Work?

It's all too easy to blame your boss for your job dissatisfaction. Indeed, there are plenty of inept managers out there. But if you've gone through the exercise in Question 12 and you think your boss would be receptive to some of the changes you'd like to make, then it's important to consider what else might be standing in your way.

Maybe you're worried that the changes won't work out or that they won't make you happier. Maybe you're worried about getting in too deep and giving yourself a ton of extra work on top of your day job. These are reasonable concerns (in fact, whatever you're worried about is a reasonable concern). But they shouldn't be reasons for continuing to wallow in misery.

If, for example, you're worried about giving yourself more work than is necessary, consider whether there's one small, easy change you can make to get started, like making client calls in the morning instead of the afternoon so as to get jazzed for the rest of the day. The point is to take your own concerns seriously and address them, instead of denying their existence or being afraid of confronting them.

14. If You're Looking for a New Job or Company, What Do You Think the New Role Will Give You That You're Not Getting from Your Current Position?

Again, we're aiming for specificity. How exactly do you imagine your work life would be different in this new, ideal role? Would you have a more congenial relationship with your boss? Would you be able to work flexibly a few days a week? Would you get paid more and have a fancier title? To say it differently, if you were to start interviewing elsewhere, what questions would you ask in order to gauge how much you'd enjoy working there?

Here's the follow-up question: Is it possible that you could get what you're looking for if you stayed at your current role? Whether the answer is yes, no, or maybe, it's critical to have that kind of clarity before you start searching elsewhere.

15. If Someone Else Were Feeling Stuck the Way You Are Right Now, What's the First Piece of Advice You Would Offer?

It's incredible how freeing a little objectivity can be. As soon as the mess isn't ours anymore, it becomes easier to see clearly how to get out of it. So imagine a friend came to you and said she really didn't like her job. Imagine she wanted your opinion (which friends don't always) on what she should do next. How would you advise her?

When I interviewed the Harvard Medical School psychologist and *Emotional Agility* author Susan David for *Insider* a few years ago, she recommended both this exercise and another in which you talk about yourself in the third person.[13] For example: "Mike is feeling lost in his career. What should he do?" As David said, "Suddenly you're kind of moving yourself from this space where you're seeing the world from the perspective of your thoughts and emotions to being able to notice them for what they are." Yes, you're confused, your emotions are saying. But that's just temporary—and we can help you get through it.

EXERCISES AND EXPERIMENTS TO IMPROVE YOUR WORKDAY

It's easy—too easy—to fall into a pattern of hating your job, assuming it's your boss's or coworkers' fault, and resigning yourself to the fact that there's nothing you can do about it. In some cases, this may be true. But in some cases, it's not. And it's worth figuring out which one of those buckets your experience falls into.

It's also important to recognize that you probably don't hate absolutely everything about your job, though you may feel that way now. Disentangling what you can't stand, what you can tolerate, and what you enjoy can be a helpful step. It will give you some clarity around what your job really looks like and how you really feel about it. From there you can make necessary change—which may involve looking for something new, but may not.

Here are some exercises for identifying what you like and dislike about your job, as well as small experiments that may help improve your work experience.

Keep a "Good Time Journal"

One of the simplest exercises I've come across for identifying what you like and dislike about your job is called the "Good Time Journal." It's the brainchild of Bill Burnett and Dave Evans, who are engineering professors at Stanford's d.school (Hasso Plattner Institute of Design) and the authors of *Designing Your Life*, *Designing Your Work Life*, and *Designing Your New Work Life*. Divide each page of your Good Time Journal into two columns. In one column, list your daily work activities; in the other column, jot down how engaged (or disengaged) you felt during each one.[14]

Burnett and Evans recommend keeping the journal for about three weeks and then doing some reflection: Did any surprising patterns emerge? You can use these fresh insights as a starting point for trying to tweak your job so that it better suits your skills and interests and/or for eventually seeking something new that allows you to do more of what you love.

Say you opt to stay in your current role and try to make it better. There are many different ways to achieve that outcome. You can choose (at least) one that seems best suited to your job situation and work environment. Remember, too, that across industries many employers are doing practically whatever it takes to keep their people happy—or to keep them, period. With workers quitting at such high rates, your organization may be more willing than you think to give you the support and resources you need and want so that you don't start looking elsewhere.

Delegate Some Projects

Another way to retool your daily work experience is by delegating some of your more loathsome responsibilities to a colleague or direct report who finds them less so. Jenny Blake, a former Googler and the founder of the Pivot Method, calls this "drafting" in her 2016 book, *Pivot*.[15] Specifically, she advises professionals looking to make a career change to ask someone they admire if they can help with any work overflow that the person doesn't have the bandwidth to handle.[16]

In this case, you'd be doing the opposite: asking a more junior colleague if they would be interested in picking up some of your projects or responsibilities. This person certainly has the option to decline, but may also jump at the chance to gain new skills and experience.

Get Rid of Tasks You Hate

Sometimes you can gradually make your worst tasks disappear. When I interviewed the authors of *Designing Your Life* for *Insider*, Burnett and Evans mentioned one professional they coached who was feeling bogged down by a specific administrative task that she assumed was part of her job. The woman tried gradually decreasing the amount of time she spent on that particular task until she wasn't doing it at all. She wasn't fired or even reprimanded. As it turned out, no one noticed.[17] That's a pretty extreme example, though I suspect it could happen in plenty of knowledge work environments where certain tasks remain part of people's job description long after those tasks have outlived their utility.

Clarify Your Career Values

Several career coaches told me that they use some version of the Values Card Sort to help clients figure out what matters in their career. (If you Google "Values Card Sort," you'll find a bunch of options.) The basic idea is that you review a list of potential values—things like autonomy, creativity, and justice—and choose the ones that most resonate with you. From there, it's easier to make career decisions that align with what's important to you.

Dissect Your Accomplishments

You may or may not want to involve your boss in the process of reshaping your role. If you do, here's a helpful exercise from Al Dea, founder of the consultancy Betterwork Labs. Dea recommends a three-step process for anyone who feels stuck and confused at work:

1. Review what you worked on and accomplished over the past two weeks. See if you can identify the most energizing and enervating activities on the list. (This is similar to the Good Time Journal.)
2. Ask yourself, "Which two or three tasks would I like to do more of to make my job better?"
3. Now ask yourself, "How might my company help me make that shift?"

At least now you'll have some concrete requests to make to your manager, or some ideas about which types of employer-sponsored programs and resources you might like to pursue.

Regardless of which strategies you choose, the broader goal is to realize that you're not trapped—or at least not as trapped as you've been feeling. For now, you may need to keep your six-figure job to provide for your family. But you don't necessarily need to keep your job exactly as it is today, soul-sucking spreadsheets and all. This does mean taking some ownership. No one's going to care about your job satisfaction like you do—not even your boss, who's busy putting out fires of his own and can't read your mind to understand how you feel about your job.

REMEMBER THIS

- Big career leaps can backfire, especially if you haven't introspected around what you really want. Sometimes a smaller, more targeted change is better.
- You can start getting unstuck in your career by asking yourself what you do and don't enjoy about your current workday and when you've felt most engaged.
- Seemingly simple strategies like delegating or even eliminating your least energizing tasks can meaningfully improve your work experience.

TRY THIS

BREAK DOWN THE BEST AND WORST PARTS OF YOUR WORKDAY

Earlier in this chapter, I introduced 15 questions that can help you clarify what's going well at work and what isn't, as well as what you most want out of your career.

I recommend answering all of them to the best of your ability. But let's start with Questions 1 and 9.

- **Question 1.** What are your favorite parts of your current workday?
- **Question 9.** What are your least favorite parts of your workday?

Write down a few answers to each question—anything from building spreadsheets to chatting with colleagues to mentoring junior staff. Keep these responses nearby while you read the rest of the book.

CHAPTER 4

DO YOU NEED TO FIND MEANING IN YOUR WORK?

THE CAREER COACH WHO SUPPORTS BORING JOBS

Lindsay Gordon brands her services as "career coaching for analytically minded people." After all, coaching has a reputation for being touchy-feely, and not especially results-oriented. In 2014, Gordon started her company, A Life of Options, for people like her, who think strategically and want to know that their time with a coach will have immediate, practical applications to their work lives.

Gordon's work caught my attention a few years ago, when I read a blog post she'd published about how it's OK to have a boring job.[1] "If it works for you and your life, a boring job can be just what you need," Gordon wrote.

It wasn't a perspective I'd heard often—as conventional wisdom goes, if you feel unfulfilled or uninspired at work, you should aim to switch to something more enlivening. But Gordon's take is that if your boring job allows you to provide for your family, or if it gives you enough free time to pursue your passions and interests (and those things are important to you), there's no pressing need to leave it. Gordon told me that when she shares this logic with her clients, they're often visibly relieved to avoid a taxing career transition that they don't really want.

What I love about Gordon's approach to career coaching is how much she emphasizes self-awareness and agency in your career. Sure, your friends (and a slew of self-help material) might be urging you to find work that's more rewarding. But ultimately, the definitions of descriptors like "rewarding" are yours to create—and the decision to pursue a new career or not is up to you.

Gordon told me that a lot of her clients show up to their first meeting with her because they feel disappointed in themselves. They'll say something about their day job like, "I'm not saving the world!" Gordon typically pauses to acknowledge their grief. Then she prompts them to really think, "What does that even mean?" Gordon told me that holding yourself to such broad standards as "saving the world" just "gives people room to beat themselves up a lot about what they are *not* doing."

From there, Gordon spends the next few sessions helping her clients craft career goals that are, in her words, "narrower but less restrictive." In other words, they're customized to the individual, *and* they give that person more freedom to find jobs that allow them to achieve that goal. If your goal is literally saving people's lives on a daily basis, there are only a few jobs out there that allow you to do that—think firefighter or emergency room physician. But if your goal is to make someone smile every day, you can probably be anything from a receptionist at a dentist's office to a certified financial planner.

This kind of reframing makes practical sense, too. After all, we can't *all* have jobs where we save lives on a daily basis. And many of us don't have any desire to do that kind of work. Even people who do pursue careers in medicine can become disenchanted with the work and want to change careers.[2] (This happened often among exhausted healthcare workers during the pandemic.[3]) There's room for everyone to build careers that suit their goals and personal preferences.

Some of Gordon's clients have come up with statements like, "I want to produce something I feel good about" or "I have a desire to impact how the world is run, surrounded by people who feel the same way." Those goals may evolve over time—and in fact, Gordon has heard many new parents say that what's important to them right now is spending time with their kids and bringing up the next generation, who will in turn contribute to the world.

Gordon's ideas about identifying what's important to you are especially relevant given that many professionals today are hungry to do work that is more "meaningful"—sometimes without knowing what that buzzword means to them. In 2018, coaching platform BetterUp released a survey that found nine in ten Americans would sacrifice part of their paycheck if they could do more meaningful work.[4]

Assuming these survey respondents were being honest, and not just saying what they thought was socially appropriate, I understand this impulse. People don't want to sit at a desk every day feeling like a cog in a wheel or like they're helping an evil corporation get richer. But do most of us know what exactly we're searching for when we say we're on a quest for greater meaning at work? Gordon encourages her clients to gain this kind of clarity by considering their unique values and strengths and how closely their current job aligns with those.

There are plenty of intensive exercises and frameworks you can use to identify your values and strengths. But for people without a lot of time on their hands, you can also take a few minutes to come up with some ideas about what "meaning" or "impact" might look like in your own career, or in the context of what you're uniquely skilled at. That will help give you some necessary clarity.

A few years ago, Gordon crunched the numbers to see how many of her clients left their jobs after being coached by her. As it turned out, more than half ended up *staying* because the shift in mindset around meaning and impact was enough to help them feel more positive about their work. "*You* get to define 'what does it look like to make a contribution,'" Gordon said. Hearing that bit of wisdom, she added, can sometimes jolt her clients out of a funk, noting that "it sets people free."

MEANINGFUL WORK: IT'S ABOUT MORE THAN JUST YOU

Even before the pandemic, there was plenty of research on the drivers of meaningful work and advice on how to choose a meaningful career. There was also some thoughtful criticism of the quest to find your life's purpose in your work. This quest can contribute to phenomena like "hustle culture"[5] and "workism"[6]—essentially the pressure to dedicate as much of your time and energy to your day job as possible.

But the pandemic accelerated the workforce's collective search for meaning. For many of us, the global crisis was a turning point that showed how fragile life can be and how you get just one chance to make your impact on the world. Articles in outlets like *Insider*,[7] the *Boston Globe*,[8] and the *Wall Street Journal*[9] described professionals at every stage of their career abandoning traditional corporate life for something they felt more connected to.

More than half of Gordon's clients stayed in their current job after considering what was most important to them in their lives.

Ideally, people would be doing work that's lucrative, that meets their lifestyle needs, and that they find personally meaningful. But we know that's not always the case. So what do you do if you've achieved expertise and financial success in a particular line of work but you don't feel that your work makes a positive impact on the world? Is it worth driving yourself up the wall every day trying to figure out what else you could do and feeling bad about not doing that?

Perhaps one big problem inherent in our search for meaningful work is that no one quite knows what meaningful work is "supposed" to look or feel like. Which means it's easy to fall into the trap of always thinking your work could be *more* meaningful, no matter whether you're a publicist, a small bookshop owner, or a veterinarian. Does bringing joy to your customers when you recommend a book by an author you know they'll love count? How about saving the life of a puppy who's just swallowed a pen cap?

To be sure, everyone defines meaningful work differently, and a person's understanding of what constitutes meaningful work will likely change over the course of that person's career. But the most succinct articulation of meaningful work I've heard so far came from Fraser-Thill, the career coach we met in Chapter 3. Meaningful work, she told me when I interviewed her for an *Insider* article in 2018, comes down to feeling like it's about more than just you.[10] Making your coworkers or clients smile counts, and so does providing for your family. Fraser-Thill told me the same thing she used to tell her students at Bates College's Center for Purposeful Work: If we expanded our definition of meaningful work, we'd have a much more satisfied workforce.

A growing body of research supports this observation, too. A study led by Wharton professor Adam Grant, author of the bestselling book *Give and Take*, found that university call center employees who met student beneficiaries of scholarships were more productive than their counterparts who didn't meet those beneficiaries.[11] And a Harvard working paper found that when cafeteria workers could see the students they were serving, they worked faster and prepared food that customers found tastier compared with a group of workers who couldn't see the students.[12] That may have to do with the fact that the cafeteria workers who could see students eating their food also said they felt more appreciated.

Studies like these suggest that one way to find greater meaning in your work is to know that your work is helping people. It goes back to Fraser-Thill's insight about seeing beyond yourself. In the case of the university call center employees and cafeteria workers, the job may literally involve, respectively, dialing alumni or frying up hamburgers. And maybe those activities are satisfying in and of themselves. But if they're not really, it helps to remember that those tasks are only the means to an end goal of making people's lives better.

Another study, led by a researcher from the WHU–Otto Beisheim School of Management, found that when women in a Mexican factory thought about how their work was benefiting their family, they performed better, even if they generally saw the work as dull.[13] The researchers write, "By reminding themselves of how their work contributes to their family lives, employees can reframe it as more meaningful and motivating."

It's as though it's easier to tolerate tedium when we can visualize the greater purpose of that tedium—in this case, supporting family members financially.

Understanding how your work benefits others can help you to reframe your job in a more positive way and even to perform better.

Seeing work as a paycheck won't necessarily make you feel great. But it helps to be able to draw the connection between a seemingly boring job and your core values, which might include caring for your family. Yes, eventually you might want something more out of your day job or your career. And that's OK. But if we're talking about ways to tolerate a job that's not so creatively stimulating, at least for the time being, it helps to remind yourself that you're *not* working in a soul-sucking vacuum.

Instead this work is a way for you to take care of the people who are most important to you.

HOW TO FIND MEANING IN MONEY

I want to go one step further in dispelling the pernicious myth that only certain types of people in certain types of jobs can do meaningful work. For that I'll turn once again to Kerri Twigg, the Manitoba-based coach (introduced in Chapter 3) who wrote the book *The Career Stories Method*. Twigg encourages her clients to think about three types of values in particular: money, status, and making a difference.[14]

As for status, Twigg advises readers to go for whichever rung on the ladder makes them happiest. She writes: "Some people are content to do their work behind the scenes. Others like to lead, but also do the work alongside colleagues in similar positions. Some people like to plan and then dictate what the next move is. Status matters."

The key is to be honest with yourself about which type of role appeals to you most—you can do meaningful work in all of them.

Twigg takes a similar stance on making a difference. "Some people are happy to have a career that allows them nice things: they can buy a car, a cottage, and donate the rest. They don't need their jobs to make a difference for a lot of people, just for people in their company or community," she writes. But "others need to make a difference in the larger world, and to be able to see that difference. They don't want to just donate to a cause, they want to be the one doing the work for that cause."

Again, figure out which type of impact-making suits you best right now, and remember that you can change people's lives in any of these capacities.

The final value Twigg addresses—money—is perhaps the most complex because it can seem gauche to care about it (or to say you care about it).

But Twigg writes in her book that it's crucial to be honest with yourself about how important money is to you and how much money you need or want right now. Once you acknowledge those preferences, you can use them to inform your career development going forward. Twigg writes that if you ignore how much you value financial freedom, you'll wind up like some of her clients, who consistently burned out and job-hopped because they kept taking roles that didn't support the kind of lifestyle they desired.

After all, wanting to earn a comfortable salary doesn't automatically make you a money-mad monster. There are plenty of other motivations that have to do with your upbringing, your personality, and other areas to potentially explore in psychotherapy. Some people just don't want to worry constantly about how they're going to pay the bills or whether they can afford to attend their friend's birthday dinner. That's not shameful—that's striving for peace of mind.

I'd also argue that being in a cushy financial situation is often what *allows* you to make a bigger social impact than you could otherwise. You can, for example, regularly donate a chunk of your earnings to a philanthropic cause of your choosing. And while writing a check to a local children's charity may not feel quite as gratifying as rolling up your sleeves and working there five days a week, anyone who does work at the charity will tell you that your financial contribution absolutely makes a difference. Not to mention that, as we saw earlier in this chapter, money allows you to provide for your family, which to many people is their most important responsibility.

Some people want to make enough money so that they don't have to worry about whether they can afford their friend's birthday dinner. Think of that as striving for peace of mind—not as shameful.

Which is to say that money can be a path to meaning, if you use that money to give your kids the ballet lessons they've been begging you for or if you donate it to your community. Money can also be a kind of meaning in and of itself if earning it allows you to finally feel independent, calm, and happy.

So if money is important to you and you're currently in a job that pays reasonably well, but you're worried that you're not making a positive impact on the world, consider two things: One, maybe your current role *is* a good fit for you right now, given your personal values. And two, maybe you can still make the kind of difference you want to make.

Though I hope this book will speed up the process, it takes some professionals years to internalize this wisdom—professionals like Danielle.

THE SOCIAL JUSTICE CRUSADER AND THE GOOD-ENOUGH GIG

Danielle had always been career-driven. But while on maternity leave with her first child, she kept calling the public relations agency where she worked to ask for more time off.

Danielle, who asked to use a pseudonym to avoid damaging her professional relationships, liked her job well enough. The pay was pretty good, too. And Danielle relished the opportunity to delve into new technologies and explain the ins and outs to reporters. "There was so much to learn," Danielle said. "It was, in a way, like being in school."

But after becoming a mother, Danielle acknowledged what she'd been subconsciously thinking for months—that this work just didn't make the kind of impact she wanted to make on the world. Danielle primarily worked with CEOs of high-growth tech startups, helping them land press coverage of their innovative products and services. She'd much rather have a similar role within a social enterprise fighting gender and racial inequities—the kind of work she'd be proud to tell this baby about one day.

Even beyond the nature of the work, the PR job was exhausting. Danielle couldn't imagine being the kind of attentive, involved mother she hoped to be if she came home every day feeling completely depleted (and still on call for any urgent emails that came in).

Working in PR was like sitting in a pressure cooker all day, racing to meet urgent (and sometimes arbitrary) deadlines. Danielle told me about one particular incident that disillusioned her about the reality of working in PR. It was 11 p.m., and Danielle was on the phone with her boss at a PR agency asking him to ease up on one of her junior colleagues who'd been crying because of the stress she was under.

"Your priorities are messed up," Danielle told her boss. Instead of taking care of his employees, he was trying to meet the unmeetable demands of an irrational client. Danielle knew this wasn't an isolated incident, either—she said it could be pervasive in PR.

So by the time Danielle was on maternity leave, she was feeling ambivalent about staying in PR. Yes, she saw a career path for herself that involved climbing the corporate ladder and becoming a VP at an agency. But she also knew how little flexibility that type of role afforded. She also wondered if helping tech startup CEOs get more attention was really the kind of impactful work she aspired to do. Danielle kept asking for more time on maternity leave, which her managers readily granted. Finally, she told them she wouldn't be returning to her position.

For the next three years or so, Danielle focused on raising her kids (she had another child shortly after the first). Then, to make some extra money while her then-husband pursued an entrepreneurial venture, she started doing subcontracting work for PR agencies and picking up some of her own clients.

"I was always in a state of tension with that feeling like, 'This is not what I want to be doing,'" she told me. The problem was that "I never did answer that question, 'Well, if you don't want to go back to that, what are you going to do?'"

When Danielle and her husband divorced, she realized just how precarious their financial situation was, having by her own admission had her "head in the sand" about their finances. Danielle went through a personal bankruptcy as she worked furiously to build her own PR business and support her two young kids.

Four years later, Danielle is 41 years old, in a new relationship, and on solid financial footing. She's still wondering about the possibility of making a career transition to something she views as more impactful. But now that she has some greater financial security, she can see her options more clearly. And her thinking around the decision to leave PR has changed somewhat.

Now, Danielle is more inclined to *stay* in the PR industry, but as an individual contributor on a team instead of a manager. That shift would presumably give her more flexibility to take care of her family. And she knows that there's work available for individual contributors, especially for skilled writers like her. She's also thinking about ways to do PR work for companies that focus on issues that are important to her, specifically mental health and financial literacy. She wonders, "How could I leverage the tech sector, where there's so much power and interest and money, for the things that I think are really important?"

Lately, Danielle is focusing less on transitioning out of PR because it's clear to her how much subject-matter expertise and earning power she's built up over the course of her career. Switching to something else that seems more personally fulfilling could mean taking a pay cut while she gets up to speed. That could be both demoralizing and impractical, since she's still supporting a young family.

She's also been meditating on the concept of meaningful work. It's something she's been craving for a long time, though she never really stopped to ask why. Now, whenever she starts feeling guilty about not doing something like nonprofit work, she reminds herself that meaningfulness "is not a human right." That might sound harsh, but Danielle tries to feel grateful for important things like her family and her romantic relationship, and for being able to pay the rent again. Coming home every day feeling like she's making the world a better place would be nice—but she told me it also seems like something of a luxury that she isn't necessarily entitled to.

Not to mention the fact that constantly fretting about whether she has the "right" job according to some arbitrary standards of meaning and impact is exhausting. "How much better is my life going to be if I wrestle with these questions?" Danielle asked. It's a dilemma she's still trying to resolve.

I'll admit that something in me lifted a little when, at the end of our second phone conversation, Danielle told me she's beginning to see her PR career as enough.

Maybe I wanted Danielle to stop feeling guilty about doing work she excels at, gets recognized for, and, at least when she has some schedule flexibility, enjoys. That kind of guilt is a heavy existential burden to bear on a daily basis. And I didn't relish the thought of Danielle, a hardworking person who cares about her family and the people around her, waking up every day and chiding herself for the life choices she's made so far.

It will be great if Danielle is able to recraft her career and do PR work for companies in the mental health and financial literacy space. But if for whatever reason that doesn't work out, I want to give Danielle and people like her a little freedom from self-flagellation. I'll say much the same thing here that I said about Ed, the university media relations director, in Chapter 2. Even if Danielle doesn't achieve her ideal career, I don't want her to feel like a failure. To all the Danielles out there in the workforce: Do the very best you can, but cut yourself some slack.

REMEMBER THIS

- There's no shame in staying at a "boring" job if it allows you to dedicate time and energy to other life priorities.
- You'll likely find your work more meaningful if you can see how it benefits people other than you.
- Don't pretend that money and status aren't important to you in your career right now if they are.

TRY THIS

DRAFT AN IMPACT STATEMENT

Pretend you're one of Lindsay Gordon's clients, and try defining meaning and impact for yourself. Remember Gordon's mantra about coming up with statements that are "narrower but less restrictive" than the common refrain, "I want to save the world."

In a LinkedIn post published in fall 2021, Gordon offered a few more examples of statements that her clients have come up with.[15] One person said that meaning and impact involve "earning money and producing something I feel good about." Another said, "I don't need to be saving the world, but I want my work to have a fast and direct impact on the consumer."

What do meaning and impact look like for you?

PART TWO

Take Action

In Part One, we explored different ways to tell our career stories and to think about agency and meaning in our careers. Part Two will introduce some tactical strategies for feeling happier and more engaged at work. You'll learn how to develop an action plan for tackling the worst parts of your workday, how to tailor your job to your specific skills and interests even without consulting your boss, and how to home in on an area of your role that resonates with you.

CHAPTER 5

DIFFERENT WAYS TO APPROACH YOUR CAREER WITH PASSION

THE BROADWAY MUSICIAN WITH JUST A JOB

If you've ever seen *The Lion King* on Broadway, you know what a spectacular production it is. I went on a class trip in fifth grade, and I can still remember the way my heart leapt as giant animals on stilts paraded down the aisles to the beat of the drums. *The Lion King* opened on Broadway in 1997, and it's the third longest running show that's still playing.

Rolando Morales-Matos has been a member of the orchestra since opening night. For the first few years he was a percussionist; then he became an assistant conductor as well.

When I called Morales-Matos one Tuesday afternoon, there was one question I really wanted the answer to: How did he keep from getting bored, or even losing his mind, playing "I Just Can't Wait to Be King" and "Can You Feel the Love Tonight" every day for 24 years? I guessed that's what would happen to me if I were in his position. Morales-Matos chuckled and told me he gets that question a lot. And he always answers the same way. "It's a job," he told me, punctuating that final word.

Morales-Matos then asked me how *I* kept boredom at bay doing the same types of interviews and writing the same types of articles every day.

The way Morales-Matos sees it, he has it pretty good. He performs six days a week, and each show runs about two hours and forty-five minutes. "On an artistic level, it's very intense," he told me. And physically it can be draining. But when he's not working, he has time to just live his life. "I want to work so I can live," Morales-Matos said. "It's very important for me to have a secure job so that I can do the things that I love doing outside of that." For Morales-Matos, those things can be as simple as having a glass of wine, smoking a cigar, and listening to BBC Radio. The list of things that help him relax definitely doesn't include music. In fact, Morales-Matos moved from Washington Heights to New Jersey many years ago because every time he came home to Washington Heights, he could hear music blasting from cars, storefronts, and teenagers' stereos on the street. He remembered screaming to himself one evening, "What the f—k! I need to freaking turn this s—t off! That's what I do for a living."

Morales-Matos also challenged my casual assumption that he plays the same exact songs six days a week. Playing music, he told me, "is like breathing." You never do it exactly the same way as the last time. On the phone, Morales-Matos gave me an example of the same set of notes that could sound just slightly different depending on where you took a rest or placed emphasis, which in turn depended on how you felt that day. *Chooka lahka chooka bing bing!* versus *Chooka lahka chooka—rest—bing!* "If you're playing the same thing over and over," Morales-Matos cautioned, "maybe there's something wrong with *you*!"

It's not just a matter of avoiding the kind of monotony that could lead to a meltdown. Morales-Matos does the kind of work that, in fact, demands creativity. You need to be someone who can listen to those two sequences above and both appreciate and enjoy the difference between them. Morales-Matos spent a decade touring with a band that he said played essentially "the same 10 tunes" everywhere the musicians went. But Morales-Matos remembers the band leader telling him, "I'm always looking for new notes." That didn't mean he was looking for new songs—it meant he was looking for the Morales-Matoses of the music world, who knew exactly how powerful a small shift like adding or deleting a rest could be.

Morales-Matos keeps interested and engaged in his music by playing the same songs slightly different each time. Any of us can do something similar in our jobs.

For Morales-Matos, music is his life's work. He's been playing percussion instruments since he was a four-year-old kid in Puerto Rico, when a teacher heard him on the drums and recognized his burgeoning talent. It's the thing he does best, the thing he knows most intimately. And because he's so skilled and experienced at it, playing percussion instruments is also the thing that pays his bills.

Outside his work on Broadway, Morales-Matos teaches at The New School, Temple University, Curtis Institute of Music, and New Jersey City University. He's been a percussionist for other ensembles including the Ron Carter Foursight Quartet, and in 2008 he released a solo album, *From the Earth*. He engages in these pursuits mostly because he loves playing music.

But the more I thought about Morales-Matos's "It's a job" remark, the more profound it sounded. Adjusting your mindset, or your expectations, around work isn't always the answer, and it won't allay everyone's discontent. Certainly, if you think that your job will fill you up completely, that you'll never wake up wishing you could just take today off, you're almost certainly heading for trouble. On the other hand, if you think of your job as something you're good at that also allows you to pay your rent and grocery bills, you'll be pleased to learn that often it can be more than that.

Morales-Matos's strategy for keeping things interesting in the pit is worth emulating, too—even for those of us who aren't musically inclined enough to find joy in playing the same notes with or without a rest in between. Morales-Matos's method for staying successful and engaged in his job is to infuse a little of himself into his daily work and to make small shifts that other people probably don't even notice.

This strategy is replicable in pretty much any profession: How can you be creative within the confines of your job, both to avoid getting sick of it and to excel at your work? For example, a corporate lawyer might generate a slightly different type of solution for the problem that every client seems to have. A salesperson might add a few new words to his usual script for a day and see how it affects sales numbers. As for me, one of the best pieces of journalism advice I've received is to think about three different ways you might tell the story you're working on. You don't have to file a spooky science fiction rendition of your feature story to your editor, but you might think about ways to sprinkle the most compelling elements of sci-fi storytelling into your article.

Ultimately, people can feel all kinds of ways about their professional lives. In fact, the same person might feel differently from one day to the next. The point is that there's no single, correct orientation toward your work. They—"they" being some sage authority on careers, perhaps—say that if you do what you love, you'll never work a day in your life. For Morales-Matos, and presumably for many other artists, that's not necessarily true. Morales-Matos has managed to craft a life and career that works for him—he makes a decent living drawing on his musical talent, and he has time to enjoy the money he earns. He's not complaining. But he's also very much looking forward to retiring in the not-too-distant future. He told me he already knows exactly what will fill his days when he hits that milestone: "Nothing."

HOW TO MAKE YOUR CAREER WORK FOR YOU

In the process of writing this book, I started asking friends and family probing questions about their careers. Did they like what they did? How did they wind up in their line of work? Why did they change jobs last year? If this isn't their dream role, what would they like to be doing instead?

Two friends—we'll call them Sam and Alexandra—had starkly different accounts of their recent career history.

Sam's Story

Sam has had the same employer for nearly a decade. He likes his job, at a national education nonprofit, well enough. And it keeps him on his toes: During busy season, he'll often have to work late nights and weekends to make sure he gets through a mountain of paperwork. But he doesn't *love* his job, at least not always. In fact, he finds much of the work monotonous and understimulating.

What matters to Sam is that the job aligns with his priorities right now, most importantly caring for his infant son. The hours are relatively flexible (aside from busy season); the pay and benefits are solid. His employer doesn't give him a hard time over taking several weeks of vacation every year. Sam gets to spend a lot of time with his family, the way other new dads in his social circle don't necessarily.

Sam told me that a decade ago, before he met his wife and certainly before he had a kid, "my priorities were probably more ambitious in the professional sense." He'd regularly attend industry conferences and networking events that could help give him a leg up professionally. He also occasionally searched for new job opportunities. Now that he has a partner and a child, he's somewhat less interested in doing that kind of schmoozing. Even if he could log onto a Zoom networking call after work (the pandemic has made in-person socializing more difficult, after all), he'd rather spend that time giving his son a bath or watching him practice crawling.

Sam is well aware of the trade-offs he might be making. "If I decided to really push myself professionally, then I would probably be at a different stratum in my professional career," he said. "I'm definitely aware of the fact that there's more out there." But he told me, "I have enough stability in my career so far" that he's OK staying where he is. He's content just to do his job and to know that his daily work is helping people.

Sam doesn't love his job, but he's good at it. And it enables him to spend time with his young family—which is very important to him at this stage in his life.

Sam calls his current approach "making my career work for me." I like that language a lot because of how much agency it attributes to him. There's a more cynical view of what Sam is doing right now, basically coasting at work while his attention is drawn to the personal stuff in his life. But Sam sees it differently: He's working as much as is necessary to keep his managers happy and, even more importantly, to serve the students who benefit from his efforts. He's been at his job 10 years already; it's not like he needs to send a few midnight emails to prove that he's a hard worker. With this in mind, Sam is actively crafting the full life he desires.

Maybe in a few years, when his son is in school, Sam will feel differently. Maybe he'll start networking again, or maybe he'll look for a new job entirely. Right now, though, Sam has a clear-eyed view of what he wants and how to configure and reconfigure the different pieces of his life to get there.

At any given time, Sam said, different things are vying for his attention: work, family, leisure. As Sam put it, "You're just trying to steer your way through to find the equation that makes you happy."

Alexandra's Story

My friend Alexandra described an approach to her career that was pretty different from Sam's.

Alexandra has worked as a Jewish educator at a few different institutions over the past decade—she gets excited about helping kids find a spiritual connection to Judaism. When I started writing this book, she was eager to tell me that, for the first time, she was working a job that *didn't* precisely align with her passions and values. On an intellectual level, she supported the nonprofit organization's mission; but it wasn't something she felt personally invested in, at least not the way her colleagues did.

"At five o'clock or six o'clock, I'm like, 'OK, I'm done.' And I close my computer," Alexandra told me. And there was something liberating in that distance, in feeling like her entire identity *wasn't* tied up in every email she sent, every presentation she gave. Alexandra's previous jobs drew very much on her passion for religious education, and she was used to a cycle of bounding out of bed in the morning and feeling depleted by the end of the day. Now she felt . . . fine, all the time.

A few months into Alexandra's job at the nonprofit, the pandemic hit. Like most of us, Alexandra started spending much of her time at home. The people she interacted with most often were her colleagues, on video chat. If this had been a different kind of job, Alexandra might have found herself entirely consumed by the work, in terms of both the amount of time she spent actively working and the amount of time she spent thinking about work.

Instead, Alexandra told me, "I found myself feeling really lost. I'm a really mission-driven person." Talking to her colleagues, "I could feel that fence between us, that absence of purpose."

The problem here, if you can call it a problem, is that Alexandra was pretty adept at the job she didn't care much about. Her supervisors knew she wasn't committed to building a career in this space the way many of them were, but they were also reluctant to lose such a high performer. She said, "I was in that weird space of: I hated my job but I was really good at it."

Alexandra came to lament the lack of purpose she felt in her job, so she took another position that she knew would be more deeply engaging and energizing.

Alexandra started searching for other opportunities and found a Jewish summer camp that was looking to hire people with her qualifications immediately. She considered the possibility of just staying at the nonprofit, coasting along, and pursuing her passions outside work hours instead. After all, Alexandra had held several jobs at summer camps before. She knew there would be crying kids, angry parents, and stressful days that seemed never-ending. Yet she also remembered how she'd coped when these things happened at other jobs: She'd feel terrible for a few minutes and then brush it off because it was just one small part of an experience she loved overall.

Ultimately, Alexandra decided to take the job at the summer camp, which primarily involved leading a youth summer program. The job was just as all-consuming and just as exhausting as she remembered. But she felt alive in a way she hadn't in two years. "I'll get yelled at [by a parent] on the phone," Alexandra told me, "but then I'm going to go find campers, and I'm going to teach them dancing because that's what I love to do." And everything would feel all right again.

There Are Different Ways to Exercise Agency in Your Career

I'm highlighting these two friends' stories because of how different they seem on the surface and how similar they are when you really dig in.

Sam has figured out how to spend just enough time on work that he can also be present with his family. Alexandra inadvertently realized that she wants an all-consuming job that she can throw herself into, so she found one. In their own ways, they're both "making their career work for them," as Sam put it. They're both exercising agency in their careers by knowing what they want and working to achieve that.

I'll say it again: People are different and want different things out of their lives and careers. People also change and want different things out of their lives and careers depending on the year or even month. The critical thing is not to do what someone else wants, even if that someone else is your past or future self.

Alexandra told me she feels privileged to pursue jobs based almost entirely on what she's passionate about. "In this one moment in my life, it's good that I don't have a family and that I'm single," she said. "I'm only responsible for myself. If I wanted to pick up and move across the country or around the world to follow my passion, I can. Because nobody else is relying on me right now."

YOU CAN LEARN TO LIKE YOUR JOB OVER TIME

Alexandra is like many other contemporary professionals, who want a job that they can invest themselves in fully and have the relative freedom to pursue their passions. And still, some of my favorite research on career development suggests that it doesn't much matter how or why you choose a job.

In 2015, when the National University of Singapore psychologist Patricia Chen was a graduate student at the University of Michigan, she and her colleagues introduced the concepts of "develop" and "fit" mindsets to explain how people achieve passion for their work.[1] The paper is a terrific look at how it's entirely possible to succeed at and enjoy your work even if it doesn't seem like a job that perfectly matches your skills and interests.

If you have a fit mindset, and most Americans do, you look for a job that suits your skills and interests right from the outset.[2] It doesn't matter as much whether the work pays well; it's more important that you enjoy it. Maybe, for example, you're a stellar coder and you could code all day, so you seek out engineering jobs at tech startups.

If you have a develop mindset, on the other hand, you believe you can take almost any job and learn to like it more over time. An example might be a recent college grad who picks up a sales job in the Macy's shoe department—even though he's not that enthusiastic about shoes—because there's an opportunity to get raises and promotions if he performs well.

The researchers wanted to know: Are workers with a fit mindset ultimately happier and more successful than those with a develop mindset, since the fit-mindset people prioritize enjoyment right from the start? Does the engineer fare better than the shoe salesperson?

The answer, they found, is a resounding no.

Working American adults who held a develop mindset ended up just as satisfied with their work—and made just as much money—as their peers who held a fit mindset. In other words, it didn't matter whether they'd chosen a job because they felt jazzed about it from day one or because it paid their bills. Years later, they all wound up feeling roughly the same way about their work.

To me, the takeaways from this research are incredibly freeing. "Although most Americans believe that passion comes from finding the right fit," the authors write, "our results suggest that this is not the only route to attain passion." In other words, there's *more than one way* to experience passion at work, not to mention more than one way to establish a lucrative career.

This is, in short, great news. Professionals at all stages of their careers face a lot of pressure to love what they do for work beyond anything else in their life. The underlying assumption is that you'll be more successful if you choose a job because it's in a line of work that lights you up.

Many employers send the message—implicitly or loud and clear—to their employees that they should be dizzy with enthusiasm for their jobs because those are the kind of people who thrive at this company. And if they realize they aren't so passionate, maybe they should look for a job elsewhere.

In some ways, this message makes sense. Most of us spend at least half our waking hours working, and no one wants to be bored or frustrated that whole time. Why would you deliberately put yourself in a position where you're doing work that means virtually nothing to you?

But as the researchers write, "Not everyone has the luxury to pick and choose the 'right' vocation." Sometimes passion is a privilege. I'd add that even if you do have the privilege to be relatively choosy about your work, there are still other motivations for selecting a career path besides immediate passion. Some people might take a job because they're good at the work, or because it pays enough that they can make a dent in their student debt. Or because the hiring managers who interviewed them seemed like a nice bunch to work alongside every day.

You should know that choosing a job for one of these reasons (or for any other) doesn't automatically doom you to a life of misery and drudgery. Especially if you go in with the attitude that passion develops over time, you might very well learn to like or care about this work.

Research shows that people can be happy and successful in a job even if it didn't appear to be a direct match for their skills and interests when they were hired.

At its core, a develop mindset is a highly proactive form of engaging with your work. Instead of waiting for the perfect role to fall off the job tree and bonk you on the head, you take almost any role that seems good enough and either mold it into something that suits you or find things about the work that do resonate with you.

That proactive molding process, by the way, doesn't require too much effort. In a chapter in the 2019 book *Passion for Work: Theory, Research, and Applications*, Chen and Phoebe Ellsworth write that college students who have a develop mindset report using a range of strategies to achieve passion for their majors.[3] Those strategies include "proactively fostering greater familiarity with their subject content, reminding themselves about how their subjects are relevant to their personal goals, and recognizing how their subjects could be applied to benefit the world at large."

The researchers write that they were surprised to find that most of these tactics, which the students came up with entirely on their own, aligned with the science on the best ways to motivate yourself. Which is to say that the students had the tools to improve their academic experience all along, just like many working professionals have the means to shape their careers.

To put it simply, you don't necessarily require professional coaching or psychological intervention to figure this out. What you really need is the confidence that comes from knowing you can help yourself.

REMEMBER THIS

- Even the most creatively demanding and rewarding jobs are often also ways to pay the bills.
- Feeling passionate about your job may matter more at some points in your career than at others.
- You can develop passion for your job over time—even if it didn't seem like a perfect match for your skills and interests at first.

TRY THIS

ASK YOURSELF WHAT'S MOST IMPORTANT IN YOUR CAREER RIGHT NOW

Recall how Sam, who works at the education nonprofit, and Alexandra, the Jewish educator, were able to get in touch with the things that matter to them in their career *right now*.

For Sam, it was having a job that lets him spend time with his family. For Alexandra, it was helping kids connect to Judaism.

What's most important in your career right now?

Remember that your answer might change in the next few years, just like it's probably changed in the last few years. That's why it's important to check in with yourself on a regular basis.

CHAPTER 6

HOW TO BREAK DOWN BARRIERS TO HAPPINESS AT WORK

THE HR HEAD AND THE MAGIC OF A TRIGGER LIST

Her dream was to become an HR head before turning 40. And by her early thirties, Shannon Sullivan was on track to make it happen.

Sullivan joined a leading company in the TV streaming industry in 2012, when the media platform was still a scrappy startup. Her first job there involved building out talent teams that either didn't exist or were struggling to gain traction. It was the kind of challenge that got her excited to go to work in the morning. It was also a challenge that she knew would bring her one step closer to that dream of running an HR team within the next few years. Sullivan's boss had been excited when she'd shared this goal with him, and he'd expressed interest in having her eventually succeed him.

But a few years into her role managing new and struggling teams, Sullivan started to feel unmotivated. Tasks like establishing companywide processes for head count and budgeting—tasks that once enlivened her—now seemed impossibly taxing. Sullivan spent a while feeling stuck, and she silently blamed the other teams she collaborated with for how lackadaisical she felt about her daily work.

Sullivan, I should add, is the kind of employee who puts her all into her work. She's the embodied definition of a "people person." Impromptu conversations and brainstorming sessions with her ambitious colleagues are what get her jazzed. Sullivan's mother and sister also work in HR, and the three of them share a passion for helping people in the modern workforce meet their potential.

At that point in her career, Sullivan really couldn't imagine that the people at her company would feel or behave differently than she did. So it was their fault, she'd mutter to herself, for their not having their act together and for her being less motivated to succeed than her team. Liking her job more was *obviously* just a matter of waiting for the people around her to be more planful and proactive. "They're in bad moods, not engaged, burned out," she said of some of her colleagues. "And I'm like, 'Man, we can only go so far, but we're held back by other teams not maturing.'"

Feeling like she was at an impasse, Sullivan started looking for similar roles at other companies. After all, she helped lead the people function in her current job, which meant that she was partly responsible for keeping employees there engaged and productive. It was only a matter of time before her personal misery started rubbing off on colleagues.

A few times a week, she took phone calls with recruiters and listened as they described the stellar perks and warm-and-welcoming work culture at their organizations. But Sullivan wasn't so easily lured into something that seemed shiny and new. She couldn't shake the nagging sense that, as she put it, "the grass wasn't greener" in these new professional pastures.

At some point Sullivan realized she was beating her head against the wall. Her colleagues weren't going to change just because she wanted them to. And if she was going to stay and advance in her job, she'd better try something to alleviate her daily misery. Sullivan started looking inward, instead of outward.

Once Sullivan started to identify "triggers" and potential solutions, she became more engaged, productive, and happier.

She realized that when she blamed another team for her frustration, "I was using that as a crutch or as an excuse instead of saying, 'It's a reality. And despite that, what's the next action I can take?'" She started reframing her thoughts: "What can we do to continue to improve and to plow through?"

Sullivan remembers the day she pulled out a notepad from her desk drawer and drew two columns: one for the "triggers" that drained her energy and made her feel like quitting and one for the simple actions she could take to address those triggers.

Trigger number one, for example, was that Sullivan's recruiting team was working with the finance team to establish basic processes for budgeting. But the folks on the finance team consistently neglected to provide the requisite information, saying they didn't have the bandwidth. Sullivan also jotted down a potential solution to this dilemma: Ask the finance team, "What resources *can* you give me?" and pinpoint the person on her team who was best equipped to navigate this interdepartmental tension with aplomb. She followed the same solution-generating process for other triggers on the list.

Almost immediately, Sullivan told me, she felt lighter. "Once I was in action on any one of those things and saw a positive result," she said, "I felt more in control." ("In action" is a term Sullivan uses often to describe the behavior of taking proactive steps to improve your work situation.) Looking back, she realizes it wasn't just her disengaged colleagues that drained her energy at work. It was the feeling of *not* being in action, just in "a vicious cycle of self-loathing."

Sullivan ultimately spent nearly eight years in her job, eventually becoming the company's HR head, just like she'd dreamed of. Today she leads the people function at the financial technology startup Dave.

She told me she rarely has to make lists of triggers and actions anymore. "It's become muscle memory," she said. When she's facing a problem, she starts experimenting with different ways to solve it. "It became that way," she said, "because I saw success in it."

HELP YOURSELF OUT OF A RUT WITH A STRATEGIC MINDSET

Recent scientific research elucidates how getting into a mental state where you're thinking about different ways to help yourself, like Sullivan did, can help you achieve your goals. Psychologists call it a "strategic mindset." In their 2020 paper on the topic, a team of researchers led by Patricia Chen at the National University of Singapore (who also coauthored the paper on fit and develop mindsets cited in Chapter 5) wrote that people with a strategic mindset will frequently ask themselves motivating questions like "What can I do to help myself?" and "How else can I do this?" and "Is there a way to do this even better?"[1]

A strategic mindset is similar in some ways to a "growth mindset," a term that was coined by developmental psychologist Carol Dweck and that's become a buzzword in corporate circles. Individuals with a growth mindset believe that they can develop their skills and abilities through hard work; they see challenges as opportunities to stretch themselves. By contrast, those with a "fixed mindset" see their skills and abilities as innate; they're interested mostly in avoiding failure. Dweck's decades of research suggest that students, athletes, and professionals with a growth mindset tend to be more successful.[2]

As for strategic mindsets, the logic around them shouldn't be so revolutionary: If you're inclined to try to help yourself, you'll get out of a rut faster than if you assume you're stuck. But in practice, how many of us engage in that kind of self-help? How many of us trust ourselves to come up with potential answers when we feel like the question is too hard?

Managers are often encouraged to have their employees generate possible solutions before approaching their boss with their problems.[3] In this case, it's a little like managing yourself: Don't go into "Woe is me" mode until you've really exhausted all your options. For example, pretend it's someone else who has the problem and you're presenting the person with some different possibilities for solving it.

I like to conceptualize the value of a strategic mindset in the context of the old wisdom about sharpening your axe. For those who aren't familiar: A man is trying and failing to chop down a tree with a blunt axe blade. Someone approaches him and asks why he doesn't just sharpen his axe and make life easier for himself. The man responds: "I can't. I'm too busy chopping down this tree."

Thinking about different ways you can make your job more satisfying is often more productive than focusing on circumstances or things you can't change.

In a knowledge worker context, imagine you're feeling stuck in your job. Say you're a bankruptcy lawyer at a fancy firm and you log long hours, but you're not especially interested in the work you're doing. In theory, you could just keep doing the work, and doing an OK job on it. After all, a corporate lawyer's daily schedule generally doesn't leave a lot of room for casual brainstorming about ways to feel happier or more motivated. And when you're feeling beaten down by your daily work experience, it's admittedly easier to think about how much you hate your boss than it is to think about the extra work *you* could do to improve things. Which is why most people blame their circumstances, Chen told me.

But what if you did take 20 minutes before diving into your workday to think about some ways to connect with these assignments so they feel more personally meaningful, or some ways to approach your boss and ask for more of the kind of projects that do resonate with you? Chen shared a few examples of broad questions you might ask yourself to kick-start this process: "What have I been doing so far?" "What else can I do help myself in this situation?" "Are there people I could reach out to for advice?"

At first it might seem like you just wasted 20 precious minutes that you could have spent working. But you might very well come up with some ideas in those 20 minutes that will help you stay more motivated. And in that case, you'd save yourself a lot of grief down the line. Not to mention you'd likely improve the quality of your work since you'd be more invested in it.

Chen told me that there are endless layers of an individual's work experience. You can choose to focus on any of these layers to feel more connected to a job you don't love. For example, you could get really good at the work so that you take a sense of pride in it and keep learning and growing. You could think about how your work is benefiting a certain community of people. You could try to find something about the work that resonates with your personal values. You could develop stronger relationships with colleagues whose company you enjoy. Chen knows these strategies are out there. It's just a matter of finding them and figuring out which one might work for you right now.

Again, this doesn't have to take a tremendous amount of time or effort. You don't need a giant piece of oaktag or a box of markers or a group of your closest friends and family members to visit your living room one evening and help you craft your career vision board. What you need is more like a few minutes every day to think about one potential fix to the issue you're facing and try it out.

As for Sullivan, the former HR head, she says the same thing to those who lament that they don't have the time or energy to reshape their job: "It's a total excuse. It's a racket." The way Sullivan sees it, those people are undoubtedly spending a lot of time and energy grumbling about how much they hate their job. They could easily channel some of these resources into coming up with possible solutions.

The same way that Sullivan appointed one of her reports to manage the relationship with the finance team, you can, for example, see about automating some of your administrative tasks. And with the minimal effort it takes to remove the obstacles to your job satisfaction, you can start to enjoy your job more.

MISERY CLUBS: HOW TO USE COMPLAINING TO YOUR ADVANTAGE

Every time I talk to people who've felt stuck at work, I ask them about the strategies they use to cope. Inevitably, they will mention their colleagues—a group of equally disgruntled comrades who gathered regularly to complain about their wrathful boss or mind-numbing assignments.

Annafi Wahed, a former consultant who now runs her own startup, used the term "misery club," which I especially like.

In her particular club, Wahed said, "We had both clients we hated and partners at our own firm we hated." She and her colleagues would complain together and vent over coffee. It was heartening just to exchange eye rolls and to know she wasn't alone in feeling like maybe she'd made a mistake coming there.

Misery clubs can be a life raft when you're feeling stuck in a job you dislike. Even if your fellow club members aren't your best friends, they're going through much the same situation that you are. And when your manager chastises you for the flaws in a seemingly perfect project report, it's a relief to hear that the manager did the same thing to someone else last week.

I'll be the first to admit: Complaining feels terrific. Sometimes there's nothing quite as cathartic as telling a friend, a romantic partner, or (perhaps best) a coworker how wretched your job is, to see the person's eyes widen and hear her say, "No way! I can't believe he did that!" So I'm certainly not advising a moratorium on complaining about work. (Bottling up your emotions and frustrations is almost always counterproductive.) What I am advising is to be more self-aware about what's going on when you're engaged in one of these venting sessions.

As Sullivan, the former HR head, alluded to, complaining can feel easier and more comfortable than stepping back and trying to think of a potential solution to the problem at hand. That's why it's important to think about how you're benefiting when you start complaining or commiserating with a colleague. Are you getting stuff off your chest so that you can breathe a little easier? Are you seeking validation in thinking your boss has gone off the deep end?

Listening to and examining your negative emotions can be the first step in changing your work experience for the better.

These are entirely reasonable motivations. But you'll want to make sure that complaining and commiserating aren't exacerbating the situation you're in, leading you to feel more demoralized or less empowered to make any substantive changes.

Susan David, the Harvard psychologist and *Emotional Agility* author we met in Chapter 3, has a terrific strategy to help frustrated professionals make the most of complaining.[4] In the book, David shares an anecdote from earlier in her career, when she was working as a technical writer in New Zealand. She didn't like the work at all, and she'd often go out to lunch with a colleague so they could vent about how horrible the job was. But as soon as she got back to the office, she writes, she'd "play nice" and keep on working.

Eventually, David realized that "[I] needed to show up to my frustration and disaffection and examine what was fueling it: chronic under-challenge." Instead of dismissing this job as a waste of her time, David writes, "I needed to do my best work, develop all the skills and contacts I could, and use this boring job to help me learn more about what I really wanted to do."

Today David encourages people in a similar position to focus on the "diagnostic piece," or to figure out what their distressing emotions are trying to tell them. "If you're someone who's moaning actively about your workplace," David told me, "you can on the one hand look at that and go, 'I'm moaning about my workplace because there's no future for me in this workplace.'" But David thinks that incessant inclination to complain "is actually a sign of hope. It is indicating to you that this is a workplace in which you see opportunity."

Even if this particular job is never going to meet your career goals and needs, the fact that you're complaining about how horrible it is suggests that you think there's a better job situation out there for you.

David also pushes frustrated professionals to dig deep into their feelings to figure out what they might mean. For example, if you're consistently bored, maybe you need more growth opportunities. David wants people to ask themselves: "What is the emotion telling me about my needs? In asking yourself that question, there's often a pathway forward."

There are a few reasons why I love David's approach. First, it's a way of making sure you aren't subsumed by your own emotions: fear, confusion, sadness, etc. Instead you're actively working with your emotions as potential pieces of data. David's approach also shows us that there's a proverbial light at the end of the tunnel—it's just a matter of being able to see it. Emotions, David is arguing, can help direct you out of a bad situation, if only you're willing to listen to them.

DISTINGUISH BETWEEN REAL AND FAKE BARRIERS TO HAPPINESS

It's easy to blame your boss, or management in general, for making your work life horrible. It's also easy to say that your boss, or your boss's boss, is the reason why you can't make any real changes that would allow you to enjoy work more. In some cases, this may be largely true. In fact, it may always be true to some extent.

But I encourage people feeling stuck and unhappy in their job to challenge their own assumptions about how much control management really has over their work experience. Sometimes—though not always—you'll find that the reason you're resistant to reshaping your role has little or nothing to do with your boss. That's what happened to me, as I described in the Preface: My editor was understanding and open to suggestions about new ways of doing things. It was more my fear of failure that was stopping me from moving forward with the stories I wanted to pitch and write. I worried that even if my editor and her editor gave me permission to write more in-depth feature stories, I'd do a terrible job with them.

This kind of plumbing of your psychic depths can be uncomfortable, for sure. (After all, I didn't do much plumbing until years later, when I was writing this book.) But the alternative is staying where you are in your job and career, continuing to feel stuck and dissatisfied.

So take a few minutes to think about two things. First come up with one or two changes you'd ideally like to make in your workday, like doing more work with clients in a certain space or doing less project management for your team. Now consider a few reasons why you *might* be hesitant to start a conversation with your manager about making these changes.

You don't need to hit on the answer that feels right immediately—just think about some potential barriers that may or may not be standing in your way. For example, are you worried that if you ask your boss about making some of these changes, you'll wind up with more work than you can handle? Are you concerned that you'll make a mistake and find out you don't enjoy working with this new type of client after all? Do you suspect that colleagues on your team will be jealous of how you were able to make these shifts?

In her 2021 book, *Trust Yourself*, career coach Melody Wilding cites indecision as a common obstacle to success for a group of individuals she calls "sensitive strivers,"[5] whom she defines as high achievers who are also more sensitive to others' behavior and their own emotions. There are plenty of ways in which they can sabotage their own professional success. Indecision is one such saboteur. Wilding describes it this way: "You can see many sides of a situation, but struggle to choose between multiple courses of action because you fear making a mistake or want to maximize your choices."

In the context of reshaping your role and improving your work life, you might constantly waver between talking to your boss about shifting your projects and avoiding the conversation entirely. You might wonder whether you would regret having the conversation. What if the conversation goes well, but then you realize you asked for the wrong things? It's as though the fear of mismanaging the job-reshaping process is paralyzing, preventing you from doing *anything* that would improve your work experience even a tiny bit.

Wilding also offers up a useful strategy called "naming and reframing." In other words, name the unhelpful thoughts in your head and then see if you can come up with a more constructive way to see the situation you're in. For example, instead of perseverating exclusively on the possibility that you ask for the wrong things, can you also consider the possibility that you ask for the *right* things and feel proud of yourself for doing so?

You can also try to anticipate issues in advance, meaning you think through what would happen if you have a conversation with your boss and then later realize you asked for the wrong things. In all likelihood, the world won't end, you won't be fired, and you won't feel any worse about work than you do right now. One solution might be talking to your boss again, explaining what you've learned, and seeing if you can go back to your old work responsibilities or try out some new ones. The more you think through different actions you can take and their most likely outcomes, the less anxious you'll feel about making some changes.

In turn, it will become harder to avoid taking action—and taking control of your work experience.

REMEMBER THIS

- You should always be thinking about ways to help yourself. As examples: Is there another way to achieve your goal? Whom can you ask for advice?
- When you find yourself complaining often about work, try to think about why you're so miserable and what your emotions might be telling you.
- Challenge the assumption that your boss is wholly responsible for the way you feel about your job.

TRY THIS

MAKE A TRIGGER-AND-ACTION LIST

We learned from Sullivan (the former HR executive) how empowering it can be to solve even a small job-related problem on your own. You can try doing the same in your own work life.

Start by writing down one "trigger," or one aspect of your job that consistently bugs you. That trigger could be something like, "My colleague interrupts me three times while I'm in the middle of focused work."

Now you'll want to write down a corresponding "action," or one thing you can do to address this issue. That action could be, "I'll wear headphones while I'm doing focused work, even if nothing is playing out of them. And if my colleague still interrupts me with a request, I'll politely say that I'll address the request as soon as I'm done with this task—but not now."

The next time that trigger pops up, see if you can follow up right away with the action you wrote down. Be sure to note how you feel afterward.

CHAPTER 7

RESHAPE YOUR ROLE

TAILOR YOUR WORK TO YOUR SKILLS AND INTERESTS THROUGH JOB CRAFTING

I'd been fascinated by the idea of job crafting ever since I interviewed Yale School of Management professor Amy Wrzesniewski for an *Insider* story in 2015.[1] Wrzesniewski told me then that job crafting should *always* be your first step when you're thinking about quitting. That's because, she said, one of two things will inevitably happen. Either you'll successfully reshape your role so that you no longer want to quit, or the process of job crafting will help you identify what you really want out of your career and you can target your job search accordingly.

Job crafting involves changing your role so it's more engaging and more meaningful to you personally. And studies have found that job crafters exist in a wide range of work environments, from hospitals to manufacturing firms. For example, researchers observed that some hospital custodians were especially motivated to serve patients and went beyond the behaviors listed in their job descriptions. They changed the art in patients' rooms and even walked visitors to the parking lot—a behavior they could have gotten fired for but that allowed them to feel they were providing comfort to people during a challenging time.[2]

Wrzesniewski's research suggests that there are three broad categories of job crafting: task crafting, relational job crafting, and cognitive crafting.[3]

- **Task crafting** involves changing the nature or number of your job responsibilities.
- **Relational job crafting** is about changing the people you interact with at work.
- **Cognitive crafting** comes down to shifting your perspective on the work you do.

Wrzesniewski assured me that job crafting doesn't have to take a lot of work on top of your day job. In fact, she said, one of the most powerful job-crafting strategies involves *pulling back* on certain tasks instead of trying to add more. If you get the sense that a certain task "is part of my job but nobody's really paying attention to whether or not it gets done or how well it's done," Wrzesniewski said, you can try either not doing it or doing a bare-bones job and seeing if anyone notices.

To be sure, in order to pull back on certain job tasks, you need to know what really matters to your boss and to the business overall. Arbitrarily scaling back on any task that seems silly will almost certainly backfire, since it's possible that it may seem silly to you but have tremendous value to upper management. If your boss or the folks in management in general haven't made their goals and priorities abundantly clear, you can generally just ask your manager what's important or what management is trying to accomplish by the end of the quarter. Consider it a form of what some career experts call "managing up," or excelling at work by learning what matters to your boss and delivering on that. That way, you, your boss, and your boss's boss are happy.

There are plenty of examples of job crafting both on and under management's radar. Wrzesniewski and her colleagues often run workshops with professionals to see the fundamentals of job crafting in action, and she's observed that workshop participants generally fall into one of two camps.

Identifying what is most important to your manager can help you eliminate some job tasks that are neither important nor engaging.

"A lot of people say, 'I can't wait to meet with my manager and talk about this,'" Wrzesniewski told me. They know, or at least suspect, that their work culture prizes employee creativity and autonomy and that their boss will be impressed by how much ownership they've taken over their role.

Other workshop participants are equally excited about the possibilities they've come up with. But they say something like, "I'm going to take this [worksheet] back to where I work; I'm going to hide it in my bottom drawer; I'm never going to say a word about it; and I'm going to begin executing it." In other words, they're going to job-craft without telling their boss, because their boss might be uptight or might be a play-by-the-rules type and unreceptive to their new ideas.

Still, in Wrzesniewski's experience, people are unlikely to get into trouble if they engage in some job crafting on their own. In fact, there's a good chance their boss won't even notice what they're doing, as long as they're still meeting expectations. When Wrzesniewski runs workshops with managers on how to cultivate job crafting among their staff, some participants say things like, "This sounds insane!" Wrzesniewski tells them, "People are doing it anyway!"

TOO MANY EMAILS, TOO FEW MEETINGS: MY EXPERIENCE WITH JOB CRAFTING

One Saturday afternoon in late fall, I joined about a dozen other professionals for a virtual workshop on job crafting.

The workshop was led by Vikki Mueller Espinosa, a 30-year Intel veteran and a volunteer helping provide free career support to employees through the Intel Corporate Mentoring Program. Espinosa had led hundreds of these workshops over the past 12 years, but her passion, she told the participants assembled in Microsoft Teams squares before her, is giving other people the tools and the confidence to "work their magic." Espinosa feels most satisfied when individual Intel employees or workshop participants experience the kind of "aha!" moment that prompts them to rethink their approach to work, whether that means shifting some tasks off their plate or changing careers entirely.

In the workshop, Espinosa first introduced the concept of task crafting, which typically involves adding, removing, simplifying, or delegating some of your job responsibilities. It didn't take long before a workshop participant clicked the "raise hand" button and asked how she could possibly explain to her boss why she wanted to eliminate one of her regular job tasks.

"It's about selling the benefits," Espinosa said. Sure, some managers might be open to hearing that the task has become mind-numbingly boring. But in most cases, Espinosa explained, you'll want to frame your request around the value that the task provides to your end users (clients, customers, readers, or whoever your end users may be).

To that end, Espinosa advised strategizing in advance so that the solution you propose benefits you, your manager, and maybe even a colleague. For example, you might ask your manager, "Is there someone else on the team who would benefit from doing this task?" Once that person has been identified, you can follow up by telling your manager how you'd prefer to spend the time you've gotten back—ideally on a business-critical project that engages you more.

I was somewhat more skeptical about cognitive crafting, or changing the way you see your role at work. When I asked Wrzesniewski about it, she told me that cognitive crafting is perhaps the most complex of the three techniques. Often, she said, it comes after making other kinds of changes. For example, it might be difficult for hospital custodians to wake up one day and start seeing themselves as "healers" as opposed to people who keep the rooms clean. Thinking this way might be considerably easier once they start interacting differently with patients and their families. It's as though they act their way into their desired role or convince themselves that this is who they are.

During the workshop, Espinosa proposed a few additional paths to cognitive crafting that struck me as both more appealing and more actionable than thinking your way to success. You can certainly focus on the social impact of your work, she said, a tactic that seemed especially relevant to a workshop participant who represented underserved students.

But you can also focus on the impact this work has on *you* and your career. Perhaps this project you're less than enthusiastic about will set you up for a promotion or give you the chance to develop a skill you'll need to get your dream job (we'll talk more about opportunities for skill development in the next chapter). Espinosa shared the example of an Intel colleague who was tasked with some tedious project management responsibilities that made her feel resentful toward her bosses. But once the colleague realized that performing these tasks would help her get noticed by upper management and possibly get promoted, it became significantly easier for her to tolerate that tedium.

In other circumstances, cognitive crafting means focusing on how your job responsibilities align with your career values. One workshop participant shared that she was rethinking a job task that caused her a considerable amount of stress—specifically writing reports that presented data in new and compelling ways—because it aligned with her value of making complex information more accessible to the general public. The more she reminded herself that drafting those reports was meeting an important career goal of hers, the less burdensome the task seemed.

The workshop ended with all of us creating our own "map" of our work life: a large piece of paper adorned with different-colored sticky notes representing our passions, values, strengths, and regular work tasks. The idea was to identify the most important roles we wanted to embody at work (to give some examples, two of Espinosa's roles are "teaching others" and "providing inspiration for growth and development") and to figure out how our passions, values, strengths, and tasks fit within those roles. Any tasks that seemed misaligned with our desired roles were to go straight in the "garage sale" section, meaning we'd need to figure out a way to get rid of them.

This mapping exercise turned out to be an enlightening experience for me. Perhaps the most significant takeaway was that I spent far too much time on email—specifically coordinating interviews with sources for stories. (That task, of course, went into my garage sale inventory.) I felt a little sheepish sharing this with the group, especially after other participants had come to seemingly more profound realizations about things like mentorship and career planning.

In crafting my job, I discovered I spent too much time on emails setting up interviews and not enough time on brainstorming with colleagues.

But it was true: Emailing back and forth with publicists and assistants was a huge time suck, and on some days it was exhausting, to the point where I barely had enough energy left to *do* the interviews or write the stories. I vowed, if only to myself, to mention this to my editor and see if we could figure out a way to automate or simplify this task so that it was less nightmarish.

I realized, too, that I was missing something most people could stand to have less of: internal meetings. Especially since the onset of the pandemic, the media has (understandably) paid a lot of attention to the general surplus of meetings and the toll it takes on workers' ability to focus and get things done. But perhaps because I'm not a manager, I wasn't suffering from the same affliction. In fact, I sometimes felt stuck or even unmotivated simply because I'd been talking to myself all day instead of bouncing ideas off colleagues or hearing from top editors what themes and story formats were resonating with our audience.

To fix this issue, I'd have to be somewhat proactive in setting up meetings with other reporters and editors across the newsroom. I'd also have to confront my fear that my colleagues would decline my invitations because they were just too busy, and focus instead on the possibility that they'd be excited to hear what was going on in another area of the newsroom.

YOUR BOSS CARES ABOUT RESULTS

Wrzesniewski told me there's never been a more opportune time to engage in job crafting than right now, when businesses are struggling to hold onto workers.

"There may be more of a sense that organizations have that they need to pay more attention to what is going to make people feel engaged," she said. Employees who stick around may find they have extra room to mold their job description. As long as you're still contributing to the company's mission and bottom line, your boss (and their boss) may not care exactly how you get there. Meaning you can be more creative in shaping your workday.

Another reason why job crafting is a more viable option today is that many leaders are shifting to a new form of performance management, which values results over how many hours people spend working.[4] Which, again, means you have more autonomy over how you get to those results.

By way of context: For a long time, too many bosses relied on their ability to see employees answering emails at their computer or taking notes during meetings in order to know if they were being productive. Other bosses overvalued "face time," showing favor to whoever got into the office early and was around to chitchat at the coffeemaker or whoever stayed late and was free to grab a beer after hours. The problem was that these bosses often discounted the importance of outcomes—what people actually produced while at their desk or in meetings.

Now that many organizations are opting for a hybrid (or in some cases, fully remote) approach, more leaders are open to different ways of evaluating performance. A July 2021 Deloitte report found that more than 65 percent of executives agreed that performance evaluations should focus more on outcomes and less on output (e.g., whether your pitch ultimately lands a new client versus how many hours you spent working on the pitch).[5]

This is a welcome change. As Emilio Castilla, a professor at the MIT Sloan School of Management, told my *Insider* colleague Aki Ito, "Measuring outcomes is a much more efficient way of measuring performance."[6]

It's also a change that may afford you the freedom to, say, work different hours so you can spend time with your family or skip some of the meetings that fall outside the scope of your role. You may also feel more empowered to answer client emails and phone calls when you can, instead of frantically checking for them every five minutes. As long as you're hitting or exceeding your targets, things like signing in at 7 a.m., showing up at every meeting, and being the most responsive person at the company may not matter very much.

To be sure, the evolution from judging employees based on how busy they look to judging them based on what they're producing will not happen overnight. And there will always be micromanager bosses who get away with their tendency to hover. But in general, this is the direction people leaders are moving in and the philosophy they're starting to endorse. It stands to benefit both overall workplaces and individual employees.

Now it's up to you to pinpoint what those optimal outcomes are, at least according to your boss. The buzzy term for this strategy, as mentioned earlier, is "managing up"—you need to figure out what's important to your boss and then deliver on those things so your boss looks good to their boss.

Perhaps the most delightful piece of managing up is that once you identify your boss's top goals and priorities, you can largely stop worrying about everything else. In turn, you may find that your job gets less overwhelming or even that it gets more satisfying because you can be confident that you're helping drive the team and the organization forward.

Ideally, you're already asking your boss about their objectives at the start of each month, quarter, or year to make sure you two are on the same page. But if you feel like you can't say for sure what your boss cares about most, you can ask your boss at any time. In an *Insider* interview, Libby Leffler, a former Facebook and Google exec, suggested framing it like this: "Here are the things I believe we should focus on for the next few months. Are these aligned with your expectations of where you think we should go?"[7]

Once you've gotten a clear picture of what's important to your manager and what specifically your manager needs from you, it will likely be easier to shut out the noise and focus on what really matters.

REMEMBER THIS

- Job crafting involves changing your role so it's more engaging and meaningful to you personally.
- Once you've identified what your managers really care about, you can start pulling back on any tasks that don't matter to them and aren't interesting to you.
- Workers have some power over their employers right now, so your boss may not care exactly how you get your work done—as long as you get it done.

TRY THIS

PLAN TO CRAFT YOUR JOB

Recall the three broad categories of job crafting that we learned about earlier in this chapter:

- **Task crafting.** Changing the nature or number of your responsibilities
- **Relational crafting.** Changing the people you interact with at work
- **Cognitive crafting.** Shifting your perspective on the work you do

Which category seems most appealing, and most feasible, to you right now? Choose one bucket and then write down one change you can make in that area.

CHAPTER 8

FIND ONE THING YOU LOVE ABOUT YOUR JOB

WHAT ONE EXECUTIVE LEARNED FROM THE BAND ON THE *TITANIC*

Eddie Lampert managed Sears by videoconference.

Though the company was headquartered in Chicago, Lampert lived in and worked from Florida and would appear on a video screen before a group of executives clustered in a conference room. With his background dark and his face glowing blue, he seemed a little like the Wizard of Oz.

Most of Sears's leadership team was cowed by Lampert's telepresence. The CEO had no compunctions about publicly chastising people—asking them smart but tough questions and then telling them how stupid they were if they didn't immediately provide the answer. Grown adults could often be seen running to their offices and breaking down in tears.

When he took a job in talent management at Sears, Dean Carter had heard it wasn't the most compassionate work environment. Once,

Sears had been the world's largest retailer. But while Carter was employed there—from 2010 to 2015—the business was fast imploding.[1] Carter took the role because he needed a job in Chicago, close to where his daughter, Grace, was attending high school. And the opportunity to practice HR at a company with roughly 120,000 employees struck him as a tantalizing challenge.

Carter told me he lost a bit of his soul working at Sears. He considered leaving the company sooner than he did so he could work someplace that was thriving, with a more humane approach to managing people. But he was certain he could learn something from such a taxing role. And he wasn't willing to take the risk of quitting before Grace graduated. Once Grace entered college, Carter and his husband could move away from Illinois, and Carter could look for a job elsewhere.

Carter said he was never the direct recipient of Lampert's ire, like most of his colleagues were. He thinks that's because he figured Lampert out early on. Carter thought Lampert was a brilliant guy, if somewhat lacking in people skills, and that it was OK to push back on him if you could back up your stance with data. He knew never to get *too* close to Lampert though, or he would risk being singed by a "volcano."

When Sears's HR head left, Lampert appointed Carter as the successor. Lampert gave Carter a thick tome, which turned out to be a guide to HR analytics (i.e., using data to manage people). Lampert's goal, he told Carter, was to make data analytics a fundamental piece of Sears's HR strategy. In fact, he told Carter he wanted him to be the top head of HR analytics in the United States.

"That began my journey," Carter said. Carter realized that each one of Sears's employees was a tremendous source of data. He could track their engagement, their job performance, and their leadership potential—and help them improve. For Carter, this was also an exciting career opportunity.

"We became the gold standard in a lot of ways for data and analytics," he said—and he and his HR team were responsible for that transformation.

One innovation Carter helped develop was designed to measure hourly workers' moods. Before clocking out at day's end, they'd choose an emoji reflecting how energetic or depleted they felt. Every day Carter's team would receive something like 72,000 responses. And this seemingly simple system turned out to be a powerful predictor of employee turnover and of store closures.

As miserable and as tumultuous as Sears's work culture was, Carter found himself excited about the analytics initiatives he was spearheading. He was energized, too, by the challenge of keeping his 11 direct reports and the 6,000 HR practitioners who worked under him engaged.

I noticed that Carter talks about his HR work with a sense of wonder, like he still can't believe he's lucky enough to be employed in this field. He also likes to describe his career experience in metaphors. The first time we met, for an *Insider* interview, he poeticized the experience of working for Sears this way: "We are the band on the *Titanic*."[2] To unpack the metaphor, the *Titanic* (Sears) is sinking, but the band (the employees) can still perform, even if just for themselves.

As Carter was building his expertise in data analytics for HR, he encouraged the members of his team to do something similar—to find a piece of their work experience that they could latch onto, something that would benefit their careers in the long run.

"Play really incredible music," Carter told the members of his team, so that regardless of whether the ship sank, they'd be stronger musicians afterward. If they ended up staying at Sears, they'd be better employees; if they moved on to another organization, they'd be greater assets to those companies, too. Carter encouraged his employees to focus on the learning experience above all: What skills did they want to acquire, and where did they want those skills to take them?

Another time, Carter told me that all 6,000 HR team members were like passengers on a life raft navigating choppy seas. You couldn't poke a hole in the raft, Carter said, or else everyone—including you—would drown. He consistently communicated to the members of his HR team that they needed to help each other—and Sears's overall workforce—get through the day and make it out of there emotionally intact. And indeed the HR team experienced surprisingly minimal turnover under Carter's leadership.

Today Carter leads the HR, finance, and legal teams at Patagonia, the outdoor apparel brand that's known worldwide for its progressive culture. (Patagonia has had onsite childcare for staffers' kids since the 1980s; employees get every other Friday off from work.) It's his dream job, and Patagonia is his ideal employer.

But he said his experience at Sears positioned him for a successful career in HR. "I'm grateful to Eddie [Lampert]," he told me in that *Insider* interview. "I learned so, so, so much." Nearly every one of Carter's 11 direct reports now leads an HR team elsewhere, thanks largely to the talent management expertise they developed at Sears.

For anyone who's miserable at work, Carter comes back to the *Titanic* imagery: Play beautiful music, regardless of the whirlwind going on around you.

"If you have to be here," he said—because you rely on the paycheck or because there are no other jobs available—"then change your framing." Find something about the work experience that you can connect to, even if the overall organizational values don't completely resonate with you.

"If we can find it at Sears, you can find it anywhere," Carter said in the *Insider* interview. "I don't mean that in a bad way. But it was a really challenging situation, and we learned a lot and grew from it. I am better as a result of my time there."

FOCUS ON YOUR LEARNING AND DEVELOPMENT

Wisdom like Carter's—play great music even if your ship is sinking; find something about the job that resonates with you—comes in handy wherever you are in your career right now. You could, theoretically, resign yourself to the possibility that your career is currently on hold because you hate your job and aren't growing in it. In this universe, you're essentially biding your time until you can leave.

Or you could do what you can to develop your skills given the circumstances.

In part this might mean seeking out new projects and leadership opportunities at your company. It might also involve a bit of a mindset shift, so that every day you remind yourself that the work you're doing now will open up better career opportunities down the road. Carter was a more attractive candidate to Patagonia because of the impactful work he'd done at Sears. You'll be more appealing to your dream employer, too.

I talked with Jessie Wisdom, a former Google people analytics manager who cofounded the HR software platform Humu, about how exactly to make this mindset shift. Humu helps employers like sweetgreen and Virgin Atlantic improve their performance and their employee engagement by sending managers and individual contributors "nudges" toward positive behavior changes. (For example, "Tell a colleague you appreciate their work.")[3]

Yet Wisdom is also aware that not all workers at every organization are ecstatic about the work they're doing or are planning to stay there forever. To workers who feel understimulated or unfulfilled by their jobs, Wisdom says, "Maybe there's something that's at least useful to your long-term learning and career prospects." In other words, even if the job responsibilities themselves don't change (or don't change much), *your focus* shifts to your own learning and development.

To use her example, say you work in a call center and find the job somewhat dull. Instead of allowing that perception to envelop the entire workday, see if you can identify one or two skills that you're developing in this job that will help you get your next job, one you really want.

That skill could be influence: As you try to persuade people to buy the product or service you're selling, think about how you're building a muscle that will come in handy whether you pursue a career in sales, marketing, or really any field that involves interacting with other people. Or say you work in consulting and regularly give presentations to other teams about your research. In this case, learning how to craft a compelling pitch will benefit you if ultimately you decide to pursue something more entrepreneurial.

Focusing on skills and tasks that enhance your career development is a good idea in any job, but particularly if you're unhappy and feel stuck in your current role.

These types of competencies—which map easily from one job or career to the next—are called "transferable skills." Being able to identify and articulate your transferable skills is critical in making a career transition, especially if you're aiming to switch industries (as opposed to switching companies in the same field).[4]

Likewise, when you're ready to make your next career move, being able to show prospective employers how much you learned and grew in your last role is a huge advantage. I've interviewed scores of HR heads and people leaders for *Insider*, and I always ask them about the top traits they're looking for in new hires. Words like "adaptability" and "learnability" come up consistently.[5]

In other words, these execs—from top employers like Microsoft, Mondelez, and Canada Goose—want candidates who are willing to learn on the job and who are excited about the challenges ahead of them. So if you can talk (genuinely) about the call center as the place where you learned the art of persuasion, and explain how that knowledge will help you in this new role you're applying for, you already have a leg up over other candidates.

Even before you make that move, you may find that identifying opportunities to learn something new or get better at a particular skill helps you feel less stuck. The social psychologist Ron Friedman, author of *The Best Place to Work*, told me in an interview for *Insider* that continuing to learn and grow is essential for feeling engaged at work.[6] The problem is, Friedman said, it's hard to feel motivated to start learning new things when you feel like your job stinks. It's a common career dilemma. So consider trying to pinpoint *one* learning opportunity on *one* day and see how you feel afterward.

For example, if you're a people manager and you want to improve at leading meetings, you might dissect a recording of a recent meeting that left you feeling inspired. What did the presenter do well, and how might you emulate those behaviors? This exercise is a way of finding something about your job that matters to you, of identifying an area where you can feel proud of yourself for making progress.

Thinking about your transferable skills and learning opportunities, Wisdom said, is about "reframing in your head the purpose of what you're doing"—and your boss doesn't even have to know about it. In fact, your boss might even be impressed when you start performing better because now you feel a stronger connection to the work. That's why an intervention like this one is ideal: It's in the best interests of you *and* your current organization.

In Wisdom's case, she told me about a rather dull job earlier in her career, before she went to grad school for behavioral decision research. Wisdom would often use her 45-minute lunch breaks to study for the GRE. That didn't exactly help with her job responsibilities, but it at least allowed her to think, "I'm working toward something else so I see a future path. Even though I know I can't do it right now and I have to stay where I am, I see a possible path out."

And that's really what focusing on your own career development will do for you: remind you that this isn't forever and that you can build your own off-ramp to something bigger and better.

Thinking this way requires putting on some metaphorical blinders. Maybe, like Carter, you're obscuring the maelstrom of your employer's or your manager's tirades. Maybe you're temporarily forgetting that this job isn't the best use of your skills or talents. Whatever you're ignoring, the idea is to just do the work. And to get really good at doing it.

I realize that this imperative goes against lots of standard career advice. For all the encouragement to think big picture, and to leisurely contemplate the gap between your life today and what you really want out of your career, there's merit in being somewhat narrow-minded. So put your head down, let the world spin around you, and become the best HR chief, or accountant, or leader in your field you can be.

DOUBLE DOWN ON YOUR STRENGTHS

Here's an important note about choosing a skill to focus on in your current role. It's OK if you aren't passionate about doing the kind of work that draws on that skill. Choosing something you're good at—or think you can *get* good at—is a solid strategy for advancing in your job and overall career.

For example, say you're using your current role as an opportunity to get better at managing Excel spreadsheets. (Yes, the skill you select can be that granular.) You don't necessarily have to *love* working in Excel, at least not right now. That love—or passion, or enjoyment, or pride—may come later on, as you improve at it.

In their 2018 book, *The Ambition Decisions*, journalists Hana Schank and Elizabeth Wallace profile women in their forties who built successful careers around the thing they were good at, even if they weren't (and maybe still aren't) entirely passionate about those things.[7]

One woman, an insurance company executive, didn't start her career as highly enthusiastic about insurance. But by the time the authors interviewed her, she'd built up significant expertise in that field, which in turn sparked passion. Another woman, a chief marketing officer at a bank, spoke "so confidently and enthusiastically about her work that we had assumed she was driven by a burning dedication to numbers, finance, or business strategy," the authors wrote. "But more likely, what we mistook for passion was actually the satisfaction of a job well done," not to mention the satisfaction of being able to support her family.

In other words (and we covered this briefly in Chapter 5, in the discussion of fit versus develop mindsets), expertise often paves the way for passion. It can feel very gratifying to be good at something. It can feel even better to be recognized as an expert in that skill, in terms of both the salary and influence you command.

Most people are happiest when their job draws on their strengths and skills. But be aware that developing a new skill set on the job can also be very fulfilling.

If you're uncertain about what specific business skill you're good at, or what you might one day be good at, you can start by identifying your strengths. A growing body of research suggests that when people do work that capitalizes on their strengths—examples include creativity, perseverance, and teamwork—they're more satisfied and more engaged.[8]

There are a number of resources (some of them free) to help you identify your strengths. Gallup has a quiz you can take, as does the positive psychology nonprofit VIA. Another option—that's possibly scarier or more convenient than an online assessment, depending on your perspective—is to ask other people what *they* think your strengths are. You can add current and former colleagues, managers, and friends and family to that list.

A few years ago, I interviewed IAC's vice president of talent Laura Sapp for *Insider*, and she told me that asking colleagues to reflect on her strengths helped her successfully pivot from executive assistant to a position on the HR team at IAC.[9] Sapp said she repeated the same process with a number of coworkers—she'd set up a time to chat, tell them she was in the process of exploring possible new roles, and then say simply, "Here's what I think I'm good at. What's your feedback?'"

Another, similar strategy for uncovering your strengths is the Reflected Best Self exercise, described in a 2005 *Harvard Business Review* article by a team of scholars at the University of Virginia, the University of Massachusetts Amherst, and the University of Michigan.[10] This exercise is similar to a 360 review, except you're focusing on your strengths and not your foibles.

First, you gather feedback from colleagues, friends, and family, specifically about your strengths and when you've displayed them. Then you look for common themes in that feedback. Last, you write a brief description of yourself, summarizing what you've learned.

The *HBR* authors cite one leader who went through this exercise and saw in his feedback experiences he'd forgotten about, "because his behavior in those situations had felt like second nature to him." In other words, self-awareness can be limited, and it can be challenging to know where you shine. Other people who know you well can help you recognize your unique value.

THINK SMALL

If you're still wondering whether a big career pivot is in order, there's a critical piece of wisdom to consider. Your job tasks typically make a bigger difference in your job satisfaction than the type of company or industry you work in.

Dane Holmes, who is the CEO of HR tech startup Eskalera and a former Goldman Sachs executive, has a useful framework to help people figure out what will truly make a difference in their engagement. Holmes divides work into three rings:

1. Your role and responsibilities
2. Your colleagues and work environment
3. Your field or industry

The most important of these three rings, according to Holmes, is your role and responsibilities. As he put it, "To be happy at your job, you have to like what you're doing on a daily basis."

For example, say you love project management. The way Holmes sees it, it probably *doesn't* matter whether you're a project manager for a tech startup or an investment bank, as long as your daily job responsibilities draw on your skills and interests. The tech startup's overall mission and purpose might be different from the investment bank's—but your workday might look very similar at either company.

Yes, it's important to connect to your organization's mission. But the eight-plus hours you spend on project management (or whatever your specific job tasks are) every day may have a bigger impact on your mood and engagement levels than the five minutes a day you spend zooming out to think about the greater import of your work. To go back to what we learned in Chapter 7: The seemingly small stuff matters.

In fact, Holmes said this logic has helped propel him forward in his own career. At Goldman, Holmes made a series of lateral moves, from global head of investor relations to global head of leadership development initiative Pine Street to global head of human capital management. He saw each move as an opportunity to keep "building things," which is what he loved most. "I was always excited about those opportunities, and that dynamic was more valuable to me than the subject matter," Holmes told me in an *Insider* interview.[11]

Holmes said the second biggest factor in your job satisfaction is the people you work with. In fact, in 2018, when Holmes was still at

Goldman, he told a group of interns that your colleagues are the *most* important thing to consider when choosing a job.[12] "Working hard feels very different when you like the people around you and when you don't," he told the interns, which is why you should seek out "a team that wants to invest in you and wants to see you do well."

The logic here is much the same: You're spending at least eight hours a day with these folks. Even if you don't necessarily connect to the organization's mission, or even if you find your work tasks understimulating, having people to laugh and commiserate with can be the difference between a great day and a terrible one.

But you can think even smaller than that.

Another way to improve your work experience in a less-than-ideal job is to remember that the workday is really a series of little experiences. You get to the office, exchange pleasantries with some colleagues, scan your inbox for pressing requests, start doing research for an assignment your boss just requested, get up for another coffee, and chat with the person you run into in the pantry. (If you work remotely, your schedule might be: Sign in, say a Slack "Good morning" to some colleagues, start doing research for that assignment, and then ping your closest coworker with a funny meme you just saw while drinking your second cup of coffee.)

So if you'd like to feel happier during the workday, it's these little experiences you'll want to target. For example, are there other colleagues whose company you enjoy and can interact with more often, say by setting up a biweekly lunch date? Can you wear headphones while doing that research so you're less likely to get interrupted and better able to focus? If you liked that assignment (and did a good job on it), can you tell your boss as much so your boss will be more inclined to give you the types of assignments that energize you from now on?

In their 2011 book, *The Progress Principle*, Harvard Business School professor Teresa Amabile and researcher and writer Steven Kramer write that "small wins" throughout the workday can have outsized impacts on our emotions. Amabile and Kramer reviewed diaries kept by workers in different industries and found that people's "immediate emotional reactions to events outstripped their *own assessments* of the event's objective importance."[13]

The small wins that Amabile and Kramer documented included a scientist who felt happier after the top technical director talked to him about a new experiment and a programmer who felt more engaged in his work as soon as he figured out how to get rid of a bug.

You can probably think of something that happened to you yesterday or the day before at work that drastically changed your mood, for better or for worse. Maybe you received a single sentence of positive—or negative—feedback from your manager on a recent assignment. Or maybe a colleague shared a template for the presentation you're currently working on, and the whole task started to seem easier. The point is that the small stuff matters—often as much as or more than the big stuff.

Too many of us, when feeling unhappy at work, look to make major career changes, like pivoting to a different industry or starting a business. And sure, sometimes these big career changes can make us happier. But they're not always necessary or advisable.

It goes back to some wisdom from Rebecca Fraser-Thill, the Portland-based career coach. When Rebecca asks her clients when in the past they felt good about what they were doing (see Chapter 3), she encourages them to look for those smaller experiences.

"They're not the things that you're touting on your LinkedIn profile," Fraser-Thill said, like your job title or rank or most recent accolade. It really is about those interactions or assignments that enlivened you, even if you wouldn't necessarily include them in your elevator pitch when someone asks what you do for a living.

I'll note here that many of the people reading this book are probably highly ambitious in their careers. In that case, the stuff on your LinkedIn profile likely *does* matter to you. That's perfectly fine, and so is wanting to advance professionally so that you earn promotions and raises and influence.

What Fraser-Thill's insights illustrate is that there are some relatively easy ways to get unstuck at work, independent of where you are in your career trajectory. In fact, you'll likely be even more motivated to earn those promotions and raises and influence when you feel happy and engaged with your work. Start small. End big.

REMEMBER THIS

- Try to find one thing about your job that resonates with you, even if the rest of the experience is dull or disappointing.
- Focusing on the skills you're developing in your current role can be helpful, especially if you believe those skills will help you land another, better job.
- Knowing you're good at your job can be gratifying in and of itself, even if the work doesn't align with your passions.

TRY THIS

IDENTIFY ONE SKILL YOU CAN DEVELOP IN YOUR CURRENT ROLE

Earlier in this chapter, we met Humu cofounder Jessie Wisdom, who advised frustrated professionals to prioritize their own learning and development.

To that end, see if you can pinpoint one skill that your current job is helping you grow. This skill can be something that will help you get your next job—one you think you'd enjoy more. Examples include so-called soft skills like public speaking and negotiation as well as more technical competencies like using PowerPoint and redlining documents.

Next, ask yourself if there are specific tasks you can do more of in your current role in order to develop this skill. Jot those down, too.

PART THREE

Give Yourself Other Options

Armed with practical tools for improving your work experience, you're now entering Part Three. You'll think about how to extract the greatest value from your current employer, how to expand your identity beyond your job title, and how to transition as cautiously as possible into something more entrepreneurial.

CHAPTER 9

EXPLORE NEW PATHS TO SUCCESS

GET MANAGEMENT TO NOTICE YOUR WORK

Al Dea is the founder of the consultancy Betterwork Labs, where he helps leaders redesign their workplaces to help employees thrive. (I introduced him briefly in Chapter 3.) But years before starting his consulting practice, he was an analyst at Deloitte.

In Dea's first year there, he felt like he was doing great, hitting all his quantitative goals and impressing his managers with his work ethic. Then annual performance reviews came around—and he was shocked to receive a lower rating than he'd anticipated.

Dea was bold enough, or maybe just desperate enough, to take one of his managers aside and ask what he might have done wrong. The manager must have seen how distraught Dea looked, because she agreed to teach him how to navigate his career so that his contributions would never go unnoticed again. The lessons he learned from that manager sparked his interest in career development and in teaching other professionals the unwritten rules of success.

The first tough lesson Dea learned: Hard work is not enough. "It's just the unfortunate world that we live in," he said. "Being able to proactively manage your career is really, really critical."

Specifically Dea learned that he needed to be his own "brand manager," meaning he was in charge of making sure other people saw and cared about his accomplishments. Otherwise, he said, even if "you do really great work, nobody knows about it."

That's especially true at large organizations (like Deloitte) where just about *everyone* is a high performer and individual accomplishments can get lost in the shuffle. Something as simple as emailing your manager at the end of the week, month, or quarter with an itemized list of what you've accomplished and how you've added value can help.

Similarly, Dea said, you'll want to know exactly how your performance is being evaluated, so you can tailor your brand management strategy and make sure you're emphasizing what the higher-ups care about. Is it sales revenue? The number of deals closed? The success of new and creative initiatives? Find out what the goals are and show how you've met them.

Dea spent the next year managing his career this way, and he was delighted to receive the top performance rating the next time around, and the time after that. Word spread to his colleagues that Dea's consulting career was taking off like a rocket ship. People started coming to him for advice, the same way he'd sought counsel from one of his managers years ago.

Understanding what you want from your career enables you to identify and pursue opportunities that will propel you forward.

Talking to these colleagues, Dea quickly realized that most people had no idea how to navigate their careers. It wasn't that they didn't care about their professional development—these were highly intelligent, educated, and ambitious people. The problem was that no one had ever told them how to do it. It was an unnecessary source of stress and anxiety for a large chunk of knowledge workers.

Dea realized, too, that if he could deconstruct career management into a series of simple steps, he could help struggling professionals all over the world feel more in control of their professional futures. In 2015, midway through his tenure at Deloitte, Dea founded MBASchooled, a platform geared specifically toward guiding prospective, current, and former business school students toward their career goals.

Dea told me that his mission—with MBASchooled and Betterwork Labs—isn't just to teach people how to hack the system so that they get the performance reviews, promotions, and raises they deserve. It's also to give them the tools to figure out what they really want out of their careers.

"If you don't have a good understanding of what it is you're actually doing," he said, "or what you're learning or how you're growing, sometimes it can be hard to spot opportunities when they come up."

It's the difference between gliding along and taking assignments that come your way and actively seeking out projects and jobs that will help you continue to build your skills and knowledge.

Dea even has a framework to help his clients do just that. He recommends pausing to reflect after every project and asking yourself the following three questions:

1. What did I do?
2. What impact or outcomes did it drive?
3. What's something new I learned from this experience?

The main purpose of this exercise is to help *you* keep track of your learning and development. But once you've gained some clarity around what you've achieved, you can also relay that information to your boss.

Now there's a term for framing your work in a way that attracts management's attention: "personal branding." It's a term that leaves a lot of people nauseated because it sounds exactly like self-promotion. But if you ask Tom Peters, who popularized the term in a 1997 *Fast Company* article, it's really about distinguishing yourself through your unique skills and knowledge.[1]

Speaking to Wendy Marx for a 2021 *Fast Company* article, Peters recommended a few paths to building your personal brand, including reading broadly and growing your professional network as much as possible.[2] Both strategies will help you pinpoint today's most pressing business problems and how your work contributes to solving them.

Ultimately, learning to be your own brand manager and understanding how performance is evaluated will help you get recognized for the value you add to your organization, just like it helped Dea get recognized. And while the nature of your job won't change, you may find that you feel a whole lot better about it.

You can draw a clear parallel between this chapter and the chapter on meaningful work. Just like it helps to know that your work is benefiting clients or customers, it also helps to know that your work is being acknowledged by your managers. In both cases, the point is to avoid feeling like you exist in a cubicle-shaped vacuum where the only person who knows or cares about your work is you. Instead you'll want to remind yourself that other people depend on you and that you and your work have unique value.

Make Your Achievements Obvious

In some cases, you may want to loop in your boss's boss when you send an email detailing your contributions. That's because this person likely has influence over whether you get a promotion or a raise—but your accomplishments can easily get lost in translation.

In an *Insider* interview, Khadijah Sharif-Drinkard, now the senior vice president for business affairs at ABC News, shared a simple strategy for getting her achievements on upper management's radar.[3] (At the time of the interview, she was the senior vice president of business and legal for BET Networks.)

Sharif-Drinkard recommends emailing your boss and your boss's boss every month, quarter, or year with an outline of your most important accomplishments. If you're a people manager, you can list your team's accomplishments as well. The point is to show how you and your reports have added value and solved problems.

In Sharif-Drinkard's case, when her boss's boss received the first email outlining what she'd been working on, he responded that he wasn't aware she was overseeing so many responsibilities!

"You have to figure out ways that you get your own voice out there so that you can translate for people what you're really doing," Sharif-Drinkard told *Insider*.

TAKE ADVANTAGE OF COMPANY RESOURCES

Sometimes it's on you to get management to notice your work. But sometimes when you're dissatisfied with your job, the best and least obvious place to get guidance is your current workplace.

Your organization may offer career development resources that can help you get unstuck—many of which will be free to you as an employee. And some organizations are ramping up these offerings amid the Great Resignation as a way of keeping existing staff engaged (and trying to prevent them from running out the door).

Consider: LinkedIn surveys found that 50 percent of executives said they expect their recruiting budget to *decrease* in 2021, while 66 percent expect their learning and development budget to stay the same or *increase*.[4] In other words, executives are planning to invest in developing their current staff, perhaps even at the expense of finding and bringing on new talent.

Meanwhile, the workforce education technology space is exploding, as companies like Walmart, Starbucks, and Disney link up with startups that help employees earn certificates and degrees in fields like cybersecurity and retail management.[5]

Here are just a few examples of career development programs run by some top startups and more established organizations:[6]

- Professional services firm KPMG runs a business school that teaches employees technical skills, business knowledge, and leadership skills.
- IBM runs an apprenticeship program that allows individuals with no technical background to earn certificates in high-demand areas such as cybersecurity and engineering.
- Bank of America partners with Columbia Business School to run the Women's Executive Development Program, which offers development sessions and leadership coaching.
- Beauty startup Glossier provides management training and leadership coaching in partnership with ThinkHuman.
- Fintech startup Brex has a Mentorship Marketplace, which pairs company leaders with employees for six months of professional development.

It's worth finding out if your employer offers anything like these and whether you're eligible to participate.

Internal Mobility

Another way to take advantage of company resources and improve your career is through internal mobility programs. "Internal mobility" simply means switching roles or teams within your current organization, and employers across industries are increasingly open to it.

According to LinkedIn data collected in 2020, internal mobility is up some 20 percent since the onset of COVID-19.[7] That's likely because employers either were hesitant to bring on new staff during a recession or couldn't find any new candidates to fill open roles once the job market got hotter. So they looked to existing talent to take on those challenges. (It's worth noting that internal mobility was becoming more common even before the pandemic. Another LinkedIn survey found that job changes within companies increased 10 percent between 2015 and 2019.[8])

In my interviews for *Insider*, I've spoken with a number of business leaders about their organization's internal mobility resources. MasterCard, for example, launched an initiative during the pandemic to match current staff with side projects that would help the company meet its goals and would help employees develop new skills.[9] Now the company has a program called Unlocked that matches employees with projects and training that align with the employees' interests.[10]

Meanwhile, Unilever uses popular talent management platform Gloat to connect employees seeking new opportunities with hiring managers looking to fill new roles.[11] Consulting firm Booz Allen Hamilton uses a similar internal system, and as of summer 2021, 98 percent of employees had completed a profile.[12]

This is all to say, if you're antsy to do something different in your day-to-day work, but aren't sure whether it's time for a big career move, the solution could be simpler than you think. Switching to a new role or team is an option that could benefit you *and* your employer.

Making the move successfully is a matter of showing how your current job skills and responsibilities are solid preparation for the new role. I'll caution that this process may require more effort and planning than you'd ideally like. For example, you may have to go through additional interviews with your prospective new managers. But it will probably take less effort and planning than moving to a new organization or industry. Not to mention, you may accelerate your career trajectory in the process.

A 2016 LinkedIn study found that professionals who have worked across job functions (for example, marketing and business development) are more likely to become executives than those who have specialized in a single area (for example, just marketing).[13] But professionals who have changed *industries* are slightly *less* likely to reach the executive level.

So if you're aiming for the C-suite, know that trying something new just might improve your chances, in addition to releasing you from the doldrums of your daily work.

Exploring a variety of roles in different departments can prepare you for a managerial career and perhaps even a C-suite position.

Perhaps that's why you'll hear plenty of business leaders and workplace experts talk about the death of the career ladder. That's the traditional path leading directly from, say, associate to vice president to managing director. Former Facebook COO Sheryl Sandberg has been credited with coining the term "career jungle gym" to describe the nonlinear trajectory that has supposedly supplanted the career ladder.[14]

Proponents of the jungle gym strategy argue that the most successful professionals hop from one department to another in search of learning opportunities, even if their next step doesn't seem like the logical upward move. Libby Leffler, the former Google and Facebook exec we met briefly in Chapter 7, described her career this way in an *Insider* interview: "I wasn't only focused on the next level up. I was really always drawn to things that intrigued me, gave me the chance to learn as much as I could, and gave me the opportunity to learn something new, with plenty of room for experimentation."[15]

To be sure, certain organizations and industries are more conducive than others to these kinds of lateral moves. You might have more room to experiment at, say, a tech company than you would at a law firm where you're trying to make partner. But I want to encourage readers not to discount the possibility of trying something new because they're afraid of derailing their career (or their earning prospects). At plenty of organizations and in plenty of industries, taking the initiative to do something different is applauded, and can lead to long-term gains in salary and prestige.

Intrapreneurship

Still another option for capitalizing on company resources is to exercise your entrepreneurial muscles within your current organization.

Even if launching a startup is your ultimate career goal, quitting your stable job to build a business from scratch isn't always possible right now. In the meantime, one path to scratching that itch while mitigating the considerable risk that comes with business ownership is "intrapreneurship." Intrapreneurs act like entrepreneurs in that they're building something entirely new, but they're working within the confines of a more established organization, meaning their employer is footing the bill for the venture.

Some companies have very explicit intrapreneurship (also called "corporate innovation") programs.[16] At Home Depot, for example, the OrangeWorks innovation lab is designed to evaluate emerging technologies that could change either the customer experience or corporate operations. It's possible that your employer might have a center for intrapreneurship, too. Or your employer might have plans to build one, in which case it's better you find out in advance and apply.

Yet even at organizations that don't have official intrapreneurship programs, there are ways to make your job more intrapreneurial. Writing in the *Harvard Business Review*, Tomas Chamorro-Premuzic, a professor of business psychology at University College London and the chief innovation officer at ManpowerGroup, offers a few potential strategies, such as focusing on selling new ideas and being more proactive instead of waiting for colleagues and managers to suggest projects.[17]

Many intrapreneurs have gone on to launch their own companies, having grown their skills and tested their ideas in a relatively low-risk context.[18] Intrapreneurship can help make your current job more exciting, too. Research suggests that employees who engage in certain types of intrapreneurial behavior—specifically creating new businesses for the organization and helping the organization keep up with industry evolutions—are more engaged at work compared with those who don't.[19]

WHAT TO DO WHEN YOU HATE YOUR BOSS

For many people, the main obstacle to taking advantage of company resources and thriving professionally is their boss. In fact, bad managers have gotten meaningfully worse during the pandemic and the resultant shift to remote and hybrid work.

HR software platform Humu assessed managers' capabilities and found that while those who ranked highest continued to do great work throughout the pandemic, managers who ranked lowest got worse—specifically at communicating, listening, and soliciting feedback.[20] Some managers weren't even aware of just how inept they were. In a 2020 report from management software provider 15Five, 84 percent of leaders reported feeling that they were successfully supporting employees during the pandemic, compared with 69 percent of employees who said the same.[21]

A manager who's inept, or who's hard to get along with, can darken your entire work experience. I spoke with someone in that very position—we'll call her Barbara—who's considering leaving her job because her bosses don't seem to acknowledge her value.

Barbara, who requested that I use a pseudonym to avoid jeopardizing her position at work, works at a small sales firm in the New York City area. She generally likes her colleagues, enjoys her work, and knows she's good at it, based on her own perception as well as sales numbers. She brings decades of industry experience. But her bosses rarely recognize her efforts or results; she hears from them much more often when they think she's done something wrong.

Barbara told me how much this disregard for her talents and contributions bothers her, enough to make her think about looking for a new role on a daily basis. "The more time I spend in that type of environment, the harder it is to maintain a good opinion of myself," she said. "Your own opinion gets worn down."

She also told me that she wishes she could be like some of her colleagues, who let their bosses' slights roll off their back instead of taking it personally. "I need to have a thicker skin," she said.

The problem is, that's not her personality. Barbara is highly sensitive to what other people are thinking and feeling—it's part of what makes her so good at her sales job. So in a way Barbara feels doubly burdened. There's her unfavorable relationship with her bosses, and there's the constant tension between how much it bothers her and how much she thinks it *should* bother her.

How to Handle a Horrible Boss

The most effective strategies for dealing with a horrible boss today aren't so different from prepandemic tactics. They're just more salient now that there are so many horrible bosses out there, many of them lacking in self-awareness. Here are a few ideas.

Seek Camaraderie

Humu found that people with bad bosses who *also* felt validation and support from their colleagues were less likely to quit than people with bad bosses who didn't have this support network.[22] At least they knew that their boss wasn't targeting them specifically and that they weren't the problem.

So don't hesitate to talk to teammates about their experiences with your boss—and even ask for their advice on dealing with tirades, or micromanagement, or flakiness. Just be sure not to fall into the trap we covered in Chapter 6, in which commiserating about work ends up making you feel worse.

Learn to Predict Your Boss's Behavior

Start paying close attention to your boss's mood and behavior—you'll quickly notice some patterns. And being able to predict when your boss will have a meltdown, or when your boss will give the green light on seemingly any request, can help you better prepare for and weather the inevitable storms.

"A lot of mistakes come from expecting people to change," Chamorro-Premuzic said. It's highly unlikely that your boss will wake up one day, realize the error of their ways, and start acting more benevolently or rationally. So stop hoping your boss will.

Instead you'll want to get a better handle on your boss's triggers. For example, does your boss seem especially irritable around the time a big project is due? Or peeved when you give a wordy presentation? Or maybe you've noticed that turning in a report late really sets your boss off. In that case, your boss probably cares about brevity and punctuality. These things might seem trivial, but being aware of them can help you avoid unnecessary conflict and grief.

Once you can anticipate your boss's irritable behavior, Chamorro-Premuzic said, "you are in a much better position to avoid it."

Minimize Interactions with Your Manager

As for Barbara, the most practical path to happiness seems to be redesigning her workday so that she interacts with her bosses as infrequently as possible.

In the meantime, she can also incorporate other coping strategies, like trying to emulate her coworkers who seem not to let their bosses' behavior bother them. It's not her natural inclination, but it's certainly one she can strengthen.

She can also start exploring other job options—a path Barbara has thus far resisted because she worries that "the devil that you know is better than the devil that you don't." (What if, she wonders, she ends up earning less money or having more conflict in her next role?)

But Barbara told me she feels most engaged when she's out in the field trying to close deals as opposed to sitting in the office with her bosses breathing down her neck.

"I feel more like myself," Barbara told me. "I feel good about myself." Barbara went on: "It hits on all the things that I enjoy. I'm a good talker, I'm fun, I'm a lively person." These qualities shine through when Barbara is on her own, so it makes sense that she should try to spend more time in that setting.

For Barbara, it won't be terribly difficult to interact less with her bosses, since her sales job doesn't require that she or her bosses sit in the office all day every day. But for those with more traditional desk jobs, it might be more practical to *add* some positive interactions with other colleagues, to balance out those distressing feelings with something lighter. (This is a form of relational job crafting, which we learned about in Chapter 7.)

Even seemingly trivial tweaks—lunching with some colleagues whose company you enjoy or scheduling a 15-minute coffee chat with a colleague whose work you admire—can meaningfully elevate your mood and feelings of self-worth.

To be sure, avoiding your bosses whenever possible is more like a Band-Aid than a solution to the root problem of managerial negligence. But if we're talking about what's within Barbara's control or yours, a Band-Aid may very well be the best bet.

REMEMBER THIS

- Sometimes hard work isn't enough. You'll also need to make sure your managers know about your achievements and the value you're adding to the business.
- Look into career development opportunities at your current organization, whether that means switching teams or participating in (free or subsidized) leadership coaching.
- Lots of people hate their boss. But if you can learn to predict your boss's behavior, you'll be in a better position to handle—and eventually avoid—your boss's blowups.

TRY THIS

DISSECT A RECENT ACHIEVEMENT

Dea shared with us three questions that you should ask yourself after completing a project. Here they are again:

1. What did I do?
2. What impact or outcomes did it drive?
3. What's something new I learned from this experience?

Think about the last project you completed at your current job. Maybe it was a report summarizing new data; maybe it was a pitch presentation with a bunch of company executives. With this project in mind, write down your answers to Dea's three questions.

Email those responses to yourself (or take a photo of the page where you wrote them by hand). They may help guide the next career development conversation you have with your manager.

CHAPTER 10

YOU ARE NOT JUST YOUR JOB

THE LAWYER WHO FOUND HER TRUE CALLING—EMERGENCY MEDICINE

Robyn Aronberg Goecke never felt the law was her calling.

She was always more interested in health and medicine; during college, she volunteered at a summer camp for children with cancer and interned at a local hospital. But becoming a lawyer seemed like a pathway to a stable career. After graduation, she pursued a joint juris doctorate and master's in public health, then spent the next 14 years practicing healthcare law, first at a national law firm and then as in-house legal counsel at two different healthcare companies in the Washington, DC, area.

For years, Goecke toyed with the idea of leaving the legal profession. It didn't really matter that the work came easily to her, someone who's smart, organized, and articulate. Even the meaningful salary that the job provided wasn't enough to make her want to stay long term. She didn't like being chained to a desk all day pushing papers, and she dreamed about going back to school to become a physician's assistant or nurse practitioner so that she could do the kind of work that really engaged her.

But it never seemed like the right time. She and her husband were raising two kids in Washington, DC, and a career pivot wouldn't happen overnight. If she chose to change careers, it could be years before she found her footing and was able to contribute to the household income again.

When Goecke finally made the decision to quit her job in 2016, her husband was at a point in his career where he could support the family on his own, at least temporarily. And both her kids were in elementary school and getting more self-sufficient every day.

Goecke spent time exploring different career options. She briefly considered taking some online courses that would prepare her to attend nursing or PA school. When her former boss called one day to gauge her interest in returning, she declined—but decided instead to start doing part-time consulting work for the company. That way, she'd have some money coming in and still have the flexibility to figure out her next move.

Consulting for her former employer quickly led to other gigs, and Goecke ended up building her own legal and consulting practice. There were days when she missed the stability of full-time employment and her colleagues' camaraderie. But she was delighted to have the freedom to craft her own schedule.

In fall 2018, Goecke got in touch with a local volunteer rescue squad and started researching what it would take to get her emergency medical technician (EMT) certification. It would be a relatively easy way to try her hand at patient care without going back to graduate school for an official degree. A few months and several hundreds of hours of training later, Goecke earned her certification. Every Wednesday night, and on some weekends, Goecke would work from 7 p.m. to 7 a.m. and take calls that were dispatched to the station from the county's 911 dispatcher. Almost immediately, she was hooked. She hadn't felt this sense of purpose and wonder since her college internships.

EMT work "satisfies an interest I've had for so long," she said. "I'm helping people." It might sound trite, but Goecke didn't often feel that way in her legal career.

Goecke told me about a recent emergency call from a woman who was having a miscarriage. When the ambulance pulled up to the woman's home, Goecke said, "I'm sure that there was a relief they felt that it was a middle-aged woman and not a 19-year-old boy who wouldn't necessarily have any perspective on what it's like to have a miscarriage."

Even though she witnesses some terrible circumstances, Goecke feels immensely grateful that she's able to help people.

"People are calling 911 when they're in a really bad situation," she said. "You are invited into this situation that they're in that could be the worst day of their life. You're there with them, and it's humbling, and you also feel this sense of gratitude that you can be there to help with that."

Rather than starting a new career, taking on a volunteer or part-time position in an area you're passionate about may provide new levels of fulfillment.

The opportunity to keep learning and developing her skills is equally exciting. Goecke recently went through training to become an ambulance driver—something she could never have imagined herself doing just a few years ago. She's also taking Spanish language classes that focus specifically on medical vocabulary so she can better treat patients whose first language is Spanish and who may not be totally fluent in English.

Goecke explained why she's immersed herself completely in emergency medicine. "I like to be busy," she told me, so much so that her husband often laughs nervously when she expresses interest in taking on yet another project. She relishes any opportunity to learn and grow as a professional and as a person.

So I asked her if she couldn't have stayed busy and taken advantage of learning opportunities in the legal world.

"Well, yes," she said. She could have enrolled in continuing legal education courses and brushed up on her Spanish to better serve clients and raised her hand for pro bono assignments. "But I think I needed something different. I don't think I would enjoy it because I would associate it with being a lawyer," she said. "I think just because it's different than my day job, it's more enticing to me."

Which is why she's planning to volunteer as an EMT for as long as possible. "Or as long as I'm physically capable," she said.

Why a Day Job Doesn't Always Cut It

There are a few critical takeaways from Goecke's career story.

One is that practicalities matter. Goecke admitted that she quit her full-time job as a lawyer only once her family was in a position to support her taking that risk. And Goecke still had her legal consulting practice even once she quit her job and started volunteering as an EMT. Her legal consulting is work that she does well and that yields a stable income, and she'd be hard-pressed to give it up.

Another lesson: Goecke is better able to tolerate doing legal work now that she can also do engaging volunteer work. She doesn't have to expend the same amount of mental energy wondering whether and how she can get back into health and medicine or whether that passion will go forever unfulfilled.

And finally, it can sometimes be easier to enjoy work when you know you're not getting paid for it. Instead you've deliberately chosen to spend your time this way, and you can stop at any point. As Goecke pointed out, she could have devised ways to keep learning and growing as a lawyer, like taking on pro bono work. But pursuing a nights-and-weekends avocation allows her to expand her identity *beyond* her day job and beyond just being a lawyer.

For Goecke, the gratification that comes with her EMT work far surpasses the satisfaction she gets from serving the needs of a legal client. "There have been calls," Goecke told me, "where the patient has said to me, 'I'm so glad you were here.'"

DO SOMETHING UNRELATED TO WORK

As Goecke learned, it will almost certainly be easier to lift some of your expectations around work if you have something else to fill those gaps. Like hobbies, or really any activities that you engage in outside of work hours. Perhaps a screenwriting class is an outlet for your creativity; or perhaps a baking club is a place to meet like-minded pals.

But if you have neither a hobby nor an inkling of where to find one, I can relate. Back in 2018, I wrote a story for *Insider* documenting my experience trying to develop some hobbies, of which I had none.[1] Over the course of a month or so, I experimented with cooking and baking, yoga and meditation, coloring in a coloring book, and writing letters by hand to friends. I enjoyed all these activities, especially the letter writing, and told my editor I *for sure* planned to keep them up.

Then I published the article and promptly ditched every single one. After all, it wasn't like I'd enrolled in a class or joined a group around any of these hobbies, meaning I had minimal accountability or motivation to continue. And when I returned home at the end of the workday, it always seemed easier to browse Twitter or watch something on television than to whip out a coloring book and crayons.

When I interviewed her for that *Insider* story, life coach Susie Moore told me it's "tragic" how many people have so little variety in their daily lives. Often, Moore said, when she asks clients what brings them pleasure or joy, they won't know how to answer. All they do aside from work is exercise, sleep, and go to the bar (though presumably even fewer people have been patronizing gyms and bars lately because of the pandemic).

But committing to a nonwork pursuit—a book club, a dance class, a painting you're planning to gift your great-aunt—can powerfully influence how happy you feel, at work and in general. Here's how.

See Tangible Progress

Laura Vanderkam, a time management expert who's authored books including *168 Hours* and *Off the Clock*, told me in an *Insider* interview that hobbies can be especially gratifying for modern professionals. That's because they allow you to make visible progress on something, which knowledge work doesn't always. Think about it: You might have a dozen cupcakes at the end of an hourlong baking class, but if you're a corporate lawyer, it might take months before you close a single deal.

Make Your Job More Tolerable

When you expand your identity to include a new hobby, you're inclined to fixate less on a single piece of it, like your job. So it's possible that you'll eventually become more tolerant of the pieces of your job you don't like. It's also possible that you'll feel less frustrated with a job that doesn't seem to make full use of your skills and passions because you'll have other, nonwork outlets for those.

"There are a wide variety of other sources of meaningfulness that people can get outside of their jobs," said Kimberly Scott, who is an assistant professor at Northwestern University's School of Education and Social Policy and an organizational effectiveness consultant and coach.

While Scott noted that social and cultural expectations encourage us to find life's meaning and fulfillment in our work, she said it's just as possible to find meaning and fulfillment outside your work, like in your family or community. You can certainly "craft your lifestyle so that you can achieve those passions and meaningfulness through that mechanism," Scott said, "as opposed to the idea that work needs to take up such a large portion of the pie."

Stop Perseverating on Work

Even if you're a relatively busy person, *adding* select activities to your calendar can be liberating. In her 2020 book, *The New Corner Office*, Vanderkam recommends scheduling a nonwork activity for the end of the day to help shift your mindset away from work.[2]

Vanderkam describes a trap she used to fall into, and it's one I often fall into myself, especially now that I've been working from home. I'll sit there with my laptop open, half checking work emails and half texting friends, so that I'm not really getting anything done and also not really getting a mental break from work.

One solution here is to essentially force yourself to close the laptop because you have another event scheduled. Earlier in Vanderkam's career, for example, she joined three community choirs so that she had a hard stop almost every workday at 6 p.m. Perhaps I should have done something similar—like enrolling in an evening class on drawing or meditation—to maintain some of my hobbies.

An activity like singing in a community choir or volunteering as an EMT can be especially meaningful for knowledge workers because it allows them a brief reprieve from *thinking* about work. And many professionals find themselves perseverating on work much of—if not all—the time. That's especially true if their work product requires some amount of deep thinking. It's even truer for those who find that the workday itself—between all the Slacks and emails coming their way—is not especially conducive to deep thinking and creativity.

Admittedly, I count myself among the professionals who think about work on a near-constant basis. It's hard for me to read any news article without being reminded of some assignment I haven't completed.

Likewise, I rarely have a conversation with a friend without generating some new story idea—especially if that friend is facing an issue at work.

Scheduling enjoyable activities to take your mind off work can help to reduce stress and avoid job burnout.

This psychological attachment to work is rarely a problem for me because I genuinely enjoy my job. In fact, it's motivated me to advance my career in ways that I might not have if I were able to fully detach from work—like committing to spend my free time writing a book on the same topics that I cover for *Insider*.

Still, there are days when I wish I could think about something, *anything*, other than my job. I know that this engagement-bordering-on-obsession can easily backfire, and sometimes I worry that I'll burn out or lose interest in writing about the workplace. I know that it would be helpful to allot some of that mental energy to a hobby or another pursuit.

EXPECT LESS FROM YOUR JOB

If further packing your schedule with some new hobbies really seems unreasonable right now, that's OK. There are still other ways to wrest your identity from the jaws of your job. One way is to expect a little less from work.

You won't necessarily change anything about your daily responsibilities, or your colleagues, or the culture around your office. Instead you'll change your *mindset*, or the way you view these job attributes.

In some ways, this shift is already under way among the general US population. A 2016 survey conducted by the Pew Research Center found that about half of employed Americans said their job was central to their identity. The other half said their job just provided a living.[3] But a 2021 Pew Research Center report found that just over 17 percent of working American adults said their job was a source of meaning, compared with 24 percent in 2017.[4] To be sure, meaning isn't the same construct as identity, but these survey results suggest that American professionals are starting to look beyond work to other sources of fulfillment.

In thinking about how to fixate less on your day job, a helpful analog is the psychology of romantic relationships. In his 2017 book, *The All-or-Nothing Marriage*, Northwestern University psychologist Eli Finkel posits that one way to improve your marriage is simply to ask less of it.[5] When you relax some of the expectations you've been placing on your marriage, Finkel says, you may find the relationship satisfies you more.

Finkel argues that contemporary marriage is typically either incredible or just OK (that's where the term "all-or-nothing" in the title comes from). That's because lots of people expect their partners to be their absolute everything: soul mate, lover, intellectual stimulation, best friend, etc. If your partner can in fact fill all these roles, your marriage is probably exhilarating. In many cases though, your partner can fill just one or two of these roles, and so you feel chronically disappointed in your partner.

But what if, Finkel suggests, you expanded the set of people you relied on to friends and family and tennis buddies? Maybe your sibling is another intellectual sparring partner, and your college roommate is another best friend. Your spouse doesn't have to do it all. And when you start thinking and behaving this way, you might start to see your spouse and the types of fulfillment your spouse *does* bring you in a new, and brighter, light.[6]

Applying Finkel's logic in a career context means you try to stop seeing your job as the sum total of your identity. You know, the activity that generates money, the pursuit that brings you personal fulfillment, the foremost outlet for your creativity, and the place where you make friends with similar interests and ambitions. Maybe your job is one or two of these things—but not all of them. For most of us, it's a more realistic perspective that's less likely to result in disappointment.

Even beyond your mindset around work, spending as much time as possible on your job is probably a bad idea. A growing body of research suggests that working 80-hour weeks, as many finance and consulting professionals in particular are wont to do, can quickly backfire. At a certain point, there are diminishing returns: You're exhausted and potentially burned out, and your work product would be significantly better if you just got some rest.[7]

To be sure, the people who most need to hear this message are executives, whose misguided philosophy of pushing yourself to the brink in order to get ahead trickles down to individual employees. Long before the pandemic, high-powered leaders like Tesla CEO Elon Musk and former Yahoo! CEO Marissa Mayer were bragging about how much they worked to get to where they are today.[8, 9] That said, I believe there's merit in reminding *everyone* that there are ways to push back against unreasonable demands that managers place on your time. Especially when you see your career choices as either quit now before this 80-hour-a-week job takes a drastic toll on your mental health or quit later, once it already has. There could potentially be a middle ground.

In fall 2021, the *Wall Street Journal* ran a popular article by Rachel Feintzeig that made the case for caring less about your work.[10] The backdrop to this article was the burnout epidemic raging across corporate America. During the pandemic, when the boundaries between home and work were blurred and when childcare was all but nonexistent, many people felt overworked and underappreciated.

Some research shows that executives who devote more energy and time to family and hobbies ultimately perform better at their jobs.

One way to avoid the fate of some of Feintzeig's sources, who had stress-induced panic attacks and heart attacks, is to work a little less. And to not worry about it—because chances are, no one except you will notice. Feintzeig spoke to Sarah Knight, the author of *The Life-Changing Magic of Not Giving a F*ck*, who estimated that up to one-quarter of your job tasks may be unnecessary.

You can reframe caring less about work and putting less effort into your job as part of identifying what you *do* care about—and shifting your behavior accordingly. Stew Friedman, emeritus professor of management practice at the Wharton School at the University of Pennsylvania, offers some enlightening research on this topic.

In 2005, Friedman and his colleagues conducted a study of 300 business professionals who started reallocating some of their time and energy toward other parts of their lives, like family, volunteer work, and self-care.[11] As it turned out, these professionals ended up performing better at their jobs, according to their colleagues. Friedman has since expanded this research to include hundreds more professionals across industries such as tech, banking, consulting, law, and medicine. (Participants are all executive MBA students at Wharton.)

"Everyone is skeptical" when they hear about this finding, Friedman told me. I certainly was. But it's possible to see it unfold in your own life if you're willing to do the hard work necessary, he said. Specifically Friedman teaches his executive MBA students how to initiate conversations with key stakeholders in their lives and careers—including spouses and kids, friends and neighbors, bosses, and clients. The critical piece is to find out what these individuals expect from you, to share what you expect from them, and to see these relationships as changeable.

In his 2008 book, *Total Leadership*, Friedman provides some direction on how to kick off these stakeholder dialogues.[12] You can start by letting them know what *you* think they expect of you. Ask them whether your perception is accurate or whether it requires some adjustment. Prompt your stakeholders for specific examples of what they need from you. And when you reflect on what they've told you, you can also offer specific examples about how you might change your behavior.

Typically, Friedman has learned that "what others expect of you is usually less than what you think they expect." And when you're able to focus on what matters to these individuals, you're less inclined to waste time on the nonessential stuff. "That's quite liberating," Friedman said.

It goes back to what we learned in Chapter 7. If you can figure out what your boss and your boss's boss value, you can probably let some other stuff fall by the wayside—and the added focus will help you achieve long-term success.

You'll also want to consider the possibility that the expectations you're struggling to meet and the judgment you're carrying around aren't coming from outside. Perhaps it's not your spouse who wants to see the laundry perfectly washed and folded every few days. And perhaps it's not your boss who wants you to respond to internal emails within seconds of receiving them. Is it conceivable that the person who demands that these outcomes are achieved and evaluates whether they've been achieved properly is . . . you?

This is not to say relaxing your own expectations will be easy. But it's important to be able to distinguish between the pressure that other people place on you and the (likely greater) pressure you place on yourself.

REMEMBER THIS

- A hobby or volunteer project can offer you new kinds of gratification, since you're choosing (i.e., not getting paid) to spend your time that way.
- Relaxing some of your expectations around work is one strategy to make a less-than-perfect job more tolerable.
- See if you can muster the courage to ask your manager, or even a key client, what they really need from you. That way you can stop wasting time on the nonessential stuff.

TRY THIS

START A CONVERSATION WITH A CAREER STAKEHOLDER

It's all but impossible to reshape your work experience on your own.

That's why you'll want to identify the key stakeholders in your career, as Wharton's Stew Friedman advised. Your stakeholders might include managers, colleagues, and clients. Choose one individual and ask that person about what they expect of you. (It's less intimidating than you might think.)

Let's say you choose your direct manager. Follow Friedman's process: Let your manager know what you think is expected of you and ask whether that perception is accurate. Then prompt your manager to give you some specific examples of what you need to do and what management would like to see from you.

Write down what you learned from that initial conversation, and think about how you feel.

CHAPTER 11

WHEN ENTREPRENEURSHIP CALLS

THE AMBIVALENT ENTREPRENEUR

When the pain in Jonathan Hunt-Glassman's stomach didn't go away after a few hours, he panicked.

He'd just come out of another one of his multiday drinking binges, and the withdrawal symptoms were starting to set in: panic attacks, fever, chills. Hunt-Glassman felt the stabbing sensation in his abdomen and assumed it was the sign of an acute liver issue caused by excessive drinking.

Hunt-Glassman made an appointment that day with a primary care provider, and he told her about his concerns. Though multiple tests and scans came back normal, the doctor recommended that Hunt-Glassman speak with one of her colleagues about his alcohol consumption.

It's still hard for Hunt-Glassman to say what exactly prompted him to take the nurse practitioner up on her offer. Hunt-Glassman was in his thirties, and he'd known he had a problem with alcohol since college. Some close friends were aware of the issue. But for the most part, Hunt-Glassman was able to fool everyone else into thinking he was fine. He was smart; he was witty; he had a demanding job as a consultant. After a night of binge drinking, Hunt-Glassman might show up to work seemingly in perfect shape, while internally he was battling severe anxiety and other hangover symptoms.

The multiday binges had started only recently. And Hunt-Glassman was under no illusions about the potential hazards of alcoholism. He knew he could wind up having seizures, even dying if he kept this up.

"Once you're in the physical symptoms of withdrawal," Hunt-Glassman told me, "you're starting to get into pretty dangerous territory."

At the doctor's office, Hunt-Glassman was honest about his drinking habits. "I felt like I was addicted to alcohol, and I wanted help in addressing that," he said. "But I was also not interested in quitting drinking entirely."

For a long time, Hunt-Glassman had assumed the only effective way to treat his alcoholism would be to go cold turkey—but he couldn't imagine never being able to grab a beer with friends or have a glass of champagne at a wedding. He knew vaguely of some medications that made you feel sick to your stomach every time you had a sip of alcohol, and he wasn't interested in those either.

To Hunt-Glassman's surprise, the doctor understood where he was coming from and prescribed Hunt-Glassman a medication called naltrexone, which helps curb the impulse to binge-drink.[1] The idea is that after you have one or two alcoholic beverages, you're not really interested in having any more. "That was a much better fit for where I was," Hunt-Glassman said.

For a few weeks he kept the pills in his medicine cabinet, unsure if he was ready to confront the issue. When he finally did take the medication, he was shocked to feel its effects almost immediately. (While some naltrexone users pair the medication with structured psychosocial support, Hunt-Glassman said he felt he had addressed the underlying drivers of his drinking problem in previous stints in therapy.)

Not long after, Hunt-Glassman went on a business trip to New Orleans. It was "a city I've done some pretty reckless things in," he said. But that evening, Hunt-Glassman was sitting and working quietly in his hotel room, getting ready to wind down for the night. And it hit him: "Whoa. This is not something that would have been possible six months ago. I feel so much better and happier, and tomorrow morning I'm not going to be racked with anxiety as I try to pull myself together for a meeting."

The proverbial wheels in Hunt-Glassman's head started turning. How come this treatment for alcoholism wasn't more widely known—and more widely used? Why were so many people suffering in vain like he had been?

The following weekend, Hunt-Glassman was headed to a wedding in the Berkshires. He and his wife were carpooling from New York with two of their friends—who just so happened to be a psychiatrist and an investor—for the three-hour drive. Hunt-Glassman realized this could be a perfect opportunity to make his pitch. Hunt-Glassman's wife and friends listened patiently as he described his idea for a business that helped alcoholics connect with doctors who could see if they were good candidates for naltrexone.

Part of the problem, Hunt-Glassman explained, was that many people with alcoholism were nervous or ashamed to tell their primary care provider about their drinking habits. So they lied and never got help. But Hunt-Glassman's business would allow patients to connect with nonjudgmental physicians they had no relationship with. That way the perceived stigma would be lessened considerably. As Hunt-Glassman described the idea in the car that morning, he said that "it was starting to feel just a little bit more real."

In the next few months, Hunt-Glassman continued to meditate on the business idea. At no point did he consider leaving his full-time job to try to get this thing off the ground— Hunt-Glassman liked consulting well enough, and he was also pretty risk averse. The thought of cutting himself off from a monthly paycheck while he toiled away on something that in all likelihood wouldn't pan out simply terrified him.

So when Hunt-Glassman found out about a startup accelerator of sorts called Tacklebox, he was intrigued. In its first iteration, Tacklebox was a program for entrepreneurs and aspiring entrepreneurs who were still employed full-time. Tacklebox didn't take equity in the startups; participants paid about $2,500 to enroll for six weeks, during which they came together a few evenings each week. The point was to learn how to test their business ideas to see if their ideas had legs—before they quit their day jobs.

Hunt-Glassman was able to explore the viability of his entrepreneurial dream, while at the same time working at a demanding job.

Hunt-Glassman enrolled in Tacklebox in summer 2019 thinking that he'd learn the basics of entrepreneurship and see if his business idea was viable. Midway through the program, he got an exciting offer to direct retail strategy for healthcare company Humana and accepted it.

That summer was a turning point in Hunt-Glassman's career. Through Tacklebox, he grew inspired to pursue his idea for a business that would help people with alcoholism, and he became even more confident that this was an innovation the world desperately needed.

At Humana, meanwhile, he dove headfirst into his job responsibilities and was pleased to work with such a nice group of colleagues. To be sure, being a high performer at Humana and trying to evaluate his business idea at the same time meant Hunt-Glassman worked almost around the clock. But he felt energized by and engaged in both types of work. He knew he couldn't keep toggling between two careers forever—but for now, it was working.

KEEP YOUR DAY JOB—FOR NOW

I covered Tacklebox a few years ago for *Insider*.[2] I read founder Brian Scordato's articles on *Fast Company* and was curious about this program that encouraged founders to take things slow (versus moving fast and breaking things). After starting three other businesses that ultimately shut down, Scordato felt the most valuable thing he could offer was guidance for other entrepreneurs who weren't sure how or even whether to pursue their business ideas. By spring 2021, Tacklebox had hosted 27 cohorts of about 10 founders each.

When Scordato reviewed applications for Tacklebox, he looked specifically for "domain expertise." In other words, what made this person the best person to start this particular company? What unique skills and knowledge did this person have that were relevant to the business area?

Anybody can have an idea for a dating app—but if you've, say, spent 15 years in app development, or if you're a social psychologist who studies romantic relationships, you're likely better positioned to execute on the idea than most other individuals.

"You should have been subconsciously preparing to build this company for a long time, in a way such that your skill sets and knowledge bases have already distanced you from any competition," Scordato told me in an *Insider* interview.[3]

I was drawn to this idea that the transition to entrepreneurship should be gradual, with lots of checkpoints along the way. There's research to support this approach, too. One University of Wisconsin study found that entrepreneurs who keep their day jobs are 33 percent less likely to fail than those who don't.[4] And an MIT study found that the average age of a successful startup founder is 45.

The study authors found that work experience explains much of the age advantage.[5] For all the stories we hear about 20-something college dropouts who made billions off their first business idea, there's merit in taking a more cautious approach to starting a company.

Around spring 2021, when the Great Resignation really kicked into gear, applications for Tacklebox "exploded," Scordato told me. Employees across industries were thinking more broadly about their career prospects, and many saw working for themselves as an attractive option. Data from the US Department of Labor indicated that the number of self-employed workers increased by 500,000 between the onset of the pandemic and November 2021.[6]

Scordato imagined Tacklebox applicants asking themselves questions like, "What am I doing?" and "Do I really want to be doing this?" and wondering if maybe working for themselves or pursuing the business idea that had been at the back of their mind for years would be a better career option.

But Scordato tried to weed out people who seemed like they were just looking for something else, *anything* else, than the job they were currently doing. The problem with applicants like this, Scordato said, is that it was more about what they didn't want to do than about the startup itself.

"There were just so many people who were like, 'Oh, I'm in finance, but I want to be a tango instructor!' We got so many applications like that."

There's nothing inherently wrong with deciding you don't want to work in finance anymore, but making the somewhat rash decision to run toward a new job because it seems utterly different from the job you have now is rarely a good idea.

Hunt-Glassman's approach to making a career change was much more thoughtful than that. Some might say he was *too* thoughtful, or too hesitant to make a final decision for fear of making a mistake. Here's how he ultimately made the transition.

THE AMBIVALENT ENTREPRENEUR MAKES A DECISION

When I first spoke to Hunt-Glassman, he was still employed at Humana and unsure of whether to make the leap to being the full-time CEO of the business he'd now officially named Oar Health. He described to me how each type of work fulfilled him in a different way and how the two types even complemented each other.

"My job at Humana builds on the skill set that I've developed over most of my career in a little bit more linear way," he said. "I value the relationships and collaboration with very talented, influential leaders in the organization," he added, and "I like the predictability and level of the compensation."

It felt like an appropriately familiar challenge, one that could catapult him to the kind of career success he'd always hoped for. Not insignificantly, it was also a way to pay for the lifestyle he'd gotten accustomed to.

On the other hand, working on Oar Health, he said, was more about "feeling as if you're shaping with your own hands something that is still very new but feels like it has tremendous potential." As an entrepreneur, he added, "the learning is in some ways greater." At the same time as he was figuring out how best to go about building a company, he was also trying to "empower and give guidance to help the UX Designers and all sorts of people with skills that are not my strong suit." Another challenge, but this time less familiar.

Hunt-Glassman had also figured out a clever way to "de-risk," in his words, his entrepreneurial activity. IAC, the multibillion-dollar conglomerate that owns brands such as Angi, Handy, Care.com, and Real Simple, had expressed interest in Oar Health. The business was now growing within an IAC incubator, which meant that IAC provided Oar Health with the financial resources necessary to get on its feet. In exchange for nearly all the equity in the business, IAC was paying Hunt-Glassman a salary.

Not every entrepreneur would be comfortable with this arrangement, since if Oar Health ever hit it big, Hunt-Glassman would never see a billion-dollar payout. But this setup worked for Hunt-Glassman because it took away some of the anxiety around investing all his time and money in a single venture that might very well implode. (Most startups eventually shut down, after all.[7]) And besides, Hunt-Glassman's primary interest in starting Oar Health was to give other people the opportunity to get better like he had, and not necessarily to become a billionaire.

In summer 2021, Oar Health hit a milestone that signaled to Hunt-Glassman it could be time to make the transition out of Humana. IAC declared that Oar Health was ready to "spin," which means it would no longer be part of the incubator and would stand on its own as an IAC-backed company.

Still, he meditated on the decision for weeks, consulting friends and mentors for their advice. "There was never any moment of revelation that made it absolutely clear what the right decision was," Hunt-Glassman told me. But it helped when he realized that even if he left Humana to join Oar Health full-time and Oar Health didn't work out, it wouldn't drastically change his career trajectory. He'd be getting solid business experience either way.

Hunt-Glassman became the full-time CEO of Oar Health in September 2021.

Hunt-Glassman's career-transition process struck me as eminently sensible and replicable. It also fits neatly with the advice I've heard from other entrepreneurs and career strategists about how to know when it's time to quit your job.

Morra Aarons-Mele, executive vice president of Geben Communications and the founder of Women Online, distinguishes between "push" and "pull" factors that motivate people to start a business. In an *Insider* interview, she explained that a push factor is hating your job and hating the idea of working for someone else. A pull factor is having a compelling business idea and being willing to risk everything to pursue it.[8]

"If I had a dollar for every time someone said to me, 'I really want to start a business because my boss doesn't let me,' I don't know, 'leave early,' 'come in late,' 'work from home' . . . ," Aarons-Mele told me in that *Insider* interview (this was before the pandemic and the era of the remote work).

"That just strikes me as really crazy and also not a great reason to start a business."

For one thing, entrepreneurship comes with tremendous challenges of its own—it's hardly a picnic. For another, there may be other bosses, teams, or jobs that let you craft your work schedule without plunging headfirst into business ownership.

In Hunt-Glassman's case, his motivations for launching Oar Health were all pull, not push. He *wasn't* trying to escape the constraints of a more traditional job. In fact, he liked his consulting gig quite a lot. Instead, he was drawn to the possibility of helping other people find their way out of a tough situation and rebuild their lives like he had.

Budding entrepreneurs should explore their motivations. It's better to be motivated by the potential of the new enterprise rather than your unhappiness in your current position.

The fact that Hunt-Glassman couldn't stop thinking about his business idea boded well for him, too. As Liz Wessel, a former Google employee who founded the startup WayUp to help entry-level workers find jobs they love, told my *Insider* colleague Áine Cain, "If you can't do a good job at your job anymore because you're spending all of your time thinking about another job opportunity, that's probably a good sign."[9] Not only are you already checked out of your current role; you also don't mind spending all your mental energy on this one idea, which you'll have to do for the foreseeable future.

But the process Hunt-Glassman used to change careers won't work for everyone. In the next section we'll meet an entrepreneur who quit her high-octane job without another role lined up.

WHEN YOUR CAREER CONSTRAINTS DISAPPEAR

Two years after graduating from college, Annafi Wahed was working at the Federal Deposit Insurance Corporation (FDIC) as a bank regulator. But her dream was to work at the Federal Reserve.

From researching the careers of current Federal Reserve employees, she noticed that many of them had first worked at fast-paced jobs in the private sector. To make herself a successful candidate for a Federal Reserve job, she'd be wise to get some similar experience.

So after roughly three years with the FDIC, Wahed left to join one of the world's most prestigious professional services firms.

For many reasons, the job was ideal. For one thing, Wahed felt that every day she was inching closer to her dream job at the Fed. The gig was also pretty cushy: At 26 years old, Wahed was earning six figures. Which was no small thing, given the thousands of dollars in student loans she'd taken out for college at Bryn Mawr.

And the job was more than a stepping-stone to another chapter in Wahed's career. It was also "intellectually interesting," she said, because it involved solving puzzles like, "How do we make sure this regulation is being implemented in a way that doesn't screw up too many things?"

Still, Wahed couldn't shake the feeling that this wasn't the way she wanted to be spending her time. Sure, those puzzles were stimulating. Wahed learned something new every day. Her managers were impressed with how swiftly she picked things up.

Meanwhile, Wahed was studying to become a chartered financial analyst (CFA), a relatively rare designation. And earning the certification would likely set her up for a promotion at work.

"But at the end of the day I felt unfulfilled," Wahed told me. Her work primarily involved working with giant banks with deep pockets. Not to mention the "insane" schedule, which meant that she didn't have much time to enjoy the hefty salary.

Wahed found herself in what she now calls an "existential crisis," pulled emotionally and psychologically in several different directions. The job paid well; the job was interesting; the job was a huge boost to her résumé. The job was also lucrative beyond anything she could have imagined at eight years old, when she arrived in the United States from Bangladesh with her mother.

"Part of her decision to bring me here," Wahed said of her mother, "was so that I could be an independent person and I wouldn't have to rely on anyone for financial security." She didn't dare tell her mother that she was even entertaining thoughts of leaving such a stable, lucrative role.

But Wahed was exhausted, and she didn't think the job wasn't making a positive difference in the world. And that last bit was getting harder and harder to ignore. "I didn't feel happy," Wahed said of working at the firm. "I felt trapped."

Starting a new company may appear glamorous, but it usually involves a lot of grunt work and an unrelenting list of mundane tasks.

While she navigated this tension between her personal values and her daily work, Wahed tried to see whether her job was salvageable. It didn't hurt that she was a top performer, which gave her an advantage when she asked for something she wanted. She told her managers she was unsatisfied with the projects she was assigned and wanted to switch to something else. In some cases, they relented. In others, they brushed her off. "Stick it out for the end of this project," Wahed remembers each one telling her, over and over again. They tried to "butter me up" with fancy dinners, as though to paper over her feelings of emptiness.

Then Wahed found out she'd passed the final CFA exam. And something shifted in the way she viewed her career. "I'd wanted to prove to everyone that I could cut it in finance," she said. "Now I have it"—the CFA charter—"this thing that so many people in finance want."

By then, she'd paid off all her student debt with the money she'd diligently saved up from the professional services firm and the FDIC. Two pressing reasons for staying at the firm—freedom from debt and the ability to slap the firm's name on her résumé—had disappeared.

Still reeling from the excitement of learning she'd passed, Wahed typed up a brief resignation letter—to have in her "back pocket," she said, for when she was emotionally ready to leave and pursue something else.

But seeing those words on paper was more powerful than she'd expected it to be. Wahed knew she was, in her words, "very employable" after stints at the FDIC and the professional services firm. Now she asked herself, "What's the worst that happens" when she walks into her boss's office and . . . quits?

It was summer 2016. The presidential election was fast approaching. Wahed remembered she had some friends from high school working on Hillary Clinton's presidential campaign. She got in touch with one of them, who told her she could easily get a job knocking on doors in either New Hampshire or Florida. The job paid, but only nominally. Wahed didn't give it more than a few seconds' thought.

She chose New Hampshire. And she submitted her two weeks' notice at the professional services firm.

Wahed quickly realized how carelessly she'd made the decision. Working in New Hampshire meant driving all day, and though Wahed technically had a license, she hadn't sat behind a wheel in a decade. Still, she felt freer than she had in years. "I was both ecstatic and terrified," she told me.

After Clinton lost the election ("It was genuinely one of the worst nights of my life," Wahed said), Wahed parlayed her political experience into founding a startup called The Flip Side, designed to show readers what both conservatives and liberals were saying about a particular issue in the news.

The day I met Wahed for lunch in Midtown Manhattan (this was summer 2021), she was feeling especially frazzled, as the team was waiting to hear back from a prominent venture capitalist about whether he was willing to make an investment. The Flip Side was on shaky financial footing, and although Wahed believed strongly in the mission, she wasn't under any illusions about its future.

"There's a 10 percent chance that I might shut down The Flip Side at the end of this year," Wahed told me. In that case, she was prepared to take a more traditional job.

People tend to "romanticize startup life or the noncorporate life," she said, as though it's this magical place where you're free from stakeholders and deadlines and stress. But as Wahed discovered, building a company from scratch involves all those things—especially stress. The experience can be worth it if you really believe you're creating something that will fundamentally improve people's lives. Still, it's not for everyone.

In fact, Morra Aarons-Mele, the Women Online founder we met earlier in this chapter, is credited with coining the term "entrepreneurship porn" to describe how aspiring founders are lured by the seeming glitz and glamour of starting a company.[10] In reality, though, building a business can be the hardest (and least glamorous) thing you ever do in your life.

Other entrepreneurship scholars told me that people can get hypnotized by the stories of founders who made it big, when in reality most businesses ultimately fail. Even businesses that thrive don't afford their founders freedom from responsibility.

"Starting a company doesn't mean being freed from the grind," Aarons-Mele wrote in the *Harvard Business Review*.[11] "It means that the buck stops with you, always, even if it's Sunday morning or Friday night."

REMEMBER THIS

- It helps to know that your startup idea is viable before you quit your job to launch a business.
- Building up technical expertise over the course of decades can prepare you to start a successful venture in that area.
- Entrepreneurship is rarely as glamorous as it seems from the outside, and it certainly won't free you from responsibility or stress.

TRY THIS

IDENTIFY YOUR PUSH AND PULL FACTORS

Recall how Morra Aarons-Mele, the Women Online founder, helps aspiring entrepreneurs break down their motivations for starting a business into "push" and "pull" factors. An example of a push factor is hating your job and never wanting to work for someone else again. An example of a pull factor is having a business idea you can't stop thinking about.

If entrepreneurship is something you're considering, draw up a list of your own push and pull factors. As you review them, see which list is longer and which factors seem the most compelling.

Aarons-Mele generally advises professionals to give more weight to their pull factors—after all, starting a business isn't the only way to get away from a micromanaging boss. But this is your decision to make. Which factors on your list tell you that starting your own business is the best career move for you right now?

CHAPTER 12

HOW TO KNOW WHEN IT'S TIME TO QUIT

DO YOU HAVE THE PERSONALITY TO QUIT?

I've mentioned a few times in this book that people are different from each other. It might sound trite, but it's incredibly easy to fall into the trap of comparing ourselves with friends, family, and colleagues—especially if their line of work is similar to ours. Why doesn't our job look as glitzy as theirs? Or why can't we muster the gumption to pivot careers the way they did last year?

There are many answers to these questions, most of which depend on the specific individuals you're talking about. Still, a near universally helpful first step is to disentangle your expectations about how you think you *should* be managing your career from how you *want* to manage your career.

I spoke about this with Alison Green, the voice behind the *Ask a Manager* website that's helped thousands of professionals navigate frustrating work dilemmas. On Green's website and in the content she writes for *New York Media* and *Vice*, she addresses questions from readers about thorny issues like hiring managers who leave you hanging and bosses who make inappropriate comments.

Since Green launched the website (then just a little blog) in 2010, she's received many letters from professionals who hate their jobs but aren't sure whether quitting is advisable.

When Green crafts advice for people in these challenging circumstances, the "People are different" rejoinder rings loud in her head. Green knows that leaving a stable job takes a certain amount of risk tolerance—and also a certain personality and attitude toward work. In other words, changing jobs and careers suits some people at some times more than others at other times.

"Maybe some people have that kind of orientation to work and some people don't," she said. "And there's no value judgment attached to that."

To some people at certain life stages, networking events, coaching workshops, and informational interviews (on top of your day job) sound absolutely thrilling. To others at other life stages, this stuff just sounds like extra work that would usurp the time they'd otherwise spend relaxing or with their family. Neither attitude is right or wrong, and neither is a permanent fixture of your work experience. People are different. People change.

It's similar to what Lindsay Gordon, the career coach and former Googler who runs A Life of Options, tells her clients about coming up with a personal definition of "impact." Self-awareness can be liberating, and practically speaking, it can save you from half-heartedly trying to switch careers when you don't really want or need that kind of upheaval in your life right now. And by the way, you don't need some wildly obvious reason for keeping things as is—a new baby, an impending divorce, hefty mortgage payments. You can be single and child-free and renting an affordable place, and if the extra work associated with changing careers feels exhausting and completely unexciting to you, *that* is a very good reason not to do it.

Regardless of your specific attitude toward work, Green told me you will have to navigate trade-offs in your career. Or as she wryly put it, deciding on a "flavor of misery" in your job. In other words, every job has downsides and reasons why you'd want to leave. It's a question of knowing which downsides you're willing to tolerate in order to gain certain upsides.

Self-awareness—understanding who you are and your life situation—is critical in deciding whether to stay in a job or pursue a new opportunity.

For example, maybe the role isn't personally fulfilling, but your employer lets you work from home or the commute to the office is easy. And so you stay. Or maybe the role is personally fulfilling, but it comes with incredibly long hours. Again, this comes down to knowing yourself and what kind of stress you're willing to tolerate—and most importantly, being honest with yourself about these things.

By her own admission, Green *is* the kind of person who relishes doing extra work—like toiling away on side projects—in order to create new career opportunities for herself. Before launching her website, *Ask a Manager*, on the tailwinds of the Great Recession, Green was the chief of staff at a nonprofit in Washington, DC. The website was a fun side project. When she quit her job at the nonprofit, Green figured she'd do blogging and freelancing for a while—and if (more like *when*, she assumed) that didn't work out, she'd get another "real" job.

It took a good deal of planning and preparation—mostly a lot of writing for *Ask a Manager*—for Green to make this career transition. Green, who was then single and in her mid-thirties, was excited about all of it. "If that stuff had felt really onerous to me at the time," she told me, "I wouldn't have done it!"

We know now that Green's transition was successful and that the *Ask a Manager* website took off. Some of that is luck, but some of it is attributable to the fact that Green invested so much of herself into the pivot. If she'd done things begrudgingly, the outcome might have been different.

Green wants her frustrated advisees to know that change is possible—it was for her. She also wants them to do what feels manageable when crafting or recrafting their careers. There's nothing wrong—or lazy—about accepting the career status quo, Green said. Again, self-awareness can be incredibly liberating.

In fact, Green told me, there's a good deal of agency to be found in knowing and accepting who you are right now. Maybe it's a relatively passive display of agency, but it's a powerful form of agency nonetheless. Sometimes, Green said, your job situation can feel easier to manage if you know you're in it deliberately.

For example, maybe you can't stand your boss. But you also know, Green said, that "I have a really short commute, I'm paid pretty well, and my benefits are great." In that case, "if you decide those are things that have made it worth staying for you, then sometimes it gets easier to deal with your very bad boss because you don't feel as helpless. You feel like you've made a clear-eyed decision to be there."

In other words, you *could* spend every hour outside of work attending industry happy hours and revising your résumé and taking a coding bootcamp—but you're not, and you don't want to, because this job pays you well enough and the benefits are decent. That's OK.

MAKE INTENTIONAL CAREER CHOICES

Most workplace experts, in fact, will want their clients to do what feels right at this juncture in their careers.

Al Dea, the Betterwork Labs founder, works often with professionals at all levels of the corporate hierarchy who say they feel stuck in their jobs.

Dea has lots of tricks up his sleeve for these individuals—career development strategies they can use to change roles, take on different projects, or simply figure out what it is that they're good at and enjoy doing.

But sometimes Dea gets pushback from his clients. "People are like, 'Holy crap! I have to do my day job and then all of this stuff?!'" Dea is always a little glad when he hears this kind of complaint. First, he reminds these clients that, no, they don't have to do any or all of the things he's recommending. There is nothing wrong with putting your head down, doing your work, and then going home (or signing off).

He also tells these clients that at least now they're starting to articulate what they *do* want. For example, maybe at this juncture in their life they'd rather spend time hanging out with their kids or learning to play the guitar instead of looking for volunteer opportunities at work. This is invaluable information.

"It forces them to think about what they want," Dea said. "What you're actually saying is that I'd rather be doing those other things." And once you've articulated that, Dea said, "now you can talk to me about those other things that you would rather be doing."

The point, he added, is to be intentional about the career choices you're making—specifically whether you're trying to speed up your career advancement, slow down, or stay right where you are. Otherwise, Dea said, "a lot of people are either on autopilot or sleepwalk." It's time to shake yourself awake.

FRAMEWORKS TO HELP YOU DECIDE WHETHER TO QUIT

In Chapter 1, I wrote that if you think there's a better job opportunity out there for you, you should take it. The chapters leading up to this one introduced a variety of ways to shift your mindset and restructure your role so that quitting isn't your *only* path to feeling happier at work. After all, part of developing and exercising agency in your work life is knowing that you have different options for advancing in your career.

If you're still considering quitting but you're unsure whether and how to make the transition, I've dedicated the next several pages to a series of frameworks that can help.

Make Sure Your Passions and Strengths Align with Your Business Needs

Patty McCord was the original chief talent officer at Netflix. (I mentioned her in Chapter 3.) I've interviewed McCord a few times for *Insider*, and she's impressed me as an incredibly clear-eyed career strategist.

In her 2018 book, *Powerful*, McCord writes that managers should always make sure that the people on their team are the right people to take the department and the company where it needs to go next.[1] But the framework she provides for managers is just as useful for individual employees considering whether *this company* is the right place to help them take their careers to the next level. Here are the three questions it boils down to:

1. Is this what I love to do?
2. Is this what I'm extraordinarily good at doing?
3. Is this something the company needs someone to be great at?

McCord told me that there are a few answer combinations that suggest you might want to consider a transition.

Sometimes, she said, "there's stuff you're really passionate about and the company just doesn't care." For example, are you fired up about fighting climate change, but management isn't really?

Other times, in McCord's words, "you've got a job you can do—you just don't love it." This scenario is similar to the dilemma my friend Alexandra described in Chapter 5: She excelled at her job responsibilities, but she just didn't feel a strong connection to the organizational mission.

(Then again, as we covered in Chapter 8, it's entirely possible to grow to enjoy doing the things you're good at.)

The final outcome, McCord said, is that "you work really hard every day, and you know it doesn't matter." Maybe you're just not skilled at this particular type of work, as much as you and your manager wish you were.

The critical piece of McCord's framework is that the answers to these questions will necessarily change *all* the time. So it's important to check in with yourself, especially when you're feeling less than enthusiastic about your role. Leaving the team or the company won't necessarily be the right answer, or the immediate answer. But at least you'll be able to start thinking of ways to reshape your work experience to get closer to the ideal.

Think Broadly About Your Options

Don't make the mistake of underestimating how many opportunities there are for you in the current job market. If you feel stuck in your current role, there are probably lots of ways to shake things up.

Tomas Chamorro-Premuzic, the professor who's appeared in this book advising readers on what to do if they hate their boss and how to act as an intrapreneur, told me that in general today's professionals "have a very narrow view of what the opportunities are." In a job search, they can easily box themselves in by looking exclusively for roles that are similar to their current one. (To be sure, as we covered in the last chapter, other professionals are looking for the opposite of their current job just because it seems different, which isn't necessarily a great idea either.)

Chamorro-Premuzic gave me an example of how this narrow kind of thinking can play out. "Most people still have very rigid concepts of their careers and their own talents," he said. If you studied journalism and have some writing experience, you might assume that you should look for editorial roles or jobs at media publications.

"You never think," Chamorro-Premuzic said, that "maybe this range of attributes, skills, and experiences could help you be a very good marketing manager," or could help you excel in another position that isn't directly related to what you've done before.

Chamorro-Premuzic's insights are especially relevant for people who work in fields where there aren't a lot of job openings right now. His insights are also valuable for people who are considering trying something new, but aren't sure what they're realistically qualified for.

Identify the Specific Risks of Quitting

A few years ago, I interviewed serial entrepreneur Harj Taggar for *Insider*.[2] Taggar was also a partner at the famed startup accelerator Y Combinator, so he has experience navigating his own transition to entrepreneurship and guiding other founders in making the same leap. Taggar told me what it was like to drop out of law school in the UK to pursue his idea for the auction and marketplace management business Auctomatic (that startup ultimately folded, but it paved the way for Taggar's subsequent entrepreneurial ventures).

At first, Taggar was consumed by the fear that dropping out of law school to start a business would be a wildly risky move that could potentially destroy his career. But then he asked himself what exactly he was concerned about. As he told me in that *Insider* interview, "What I pushed myself on was, 'OK, what is the big risk here?'" At the time, Taggar had minimal savings. But as a young, single man, he also had relatively few expenses. He remembers the dawning realization that "the worst-case scenario here is, I work on a startup, it doesn't go anywhere, and 12 months later, I re-enroll in law school."

Once he could see things more clearly, he quit law school to move to the United States and go all-in on his startup idea. Today, when he advises aspiring startup founders, or really any professionals thinking about their next career move, he tells them, "Be specific. What exactly is the risk?"

If you're concerned that you won't be able to put food on the table for your family, well, that's a big risk that you might not be comfortable taking. But if, like Taggar, your lifestyle can withstand a period of tumult or unpredictability, maybe that's not so intimidating. The point is to know the possible costs of the decision and make the choice intentionally, instead of staying afraid of a blob you can't quite see the shape of.

Assess Your Current Life and Career Circumstances

Josh Bersin, a leading HR industry analyst, always encourages introspection—even if you think you know what you want out of your career. Here are some prompts that can help:

1. What do you like to do?
2. What are you good at?

Bersin said your answers to Questions 1 and 2 will often overlap. It goes back to what we learned in the last chapter—your strengths can quickly become your passions.

And now consider Question 3:

3. What are your career aspirations *right now*?

Maybe you're at a point in your life where you're responsible for just you and you don't have many financial constraints—and you want to drive full-speed ahead toward your professional goals. Or maybe you just started a family and bought a house, and you're disinclined to take a new and high-stress role. Your career aspirations may differ markedly at these two different life stages.

Do the Gun Test

You can agonize forever over the decision to quit your job. Even if you decide to leave for something else, you may never be entirely certain that leaving was the right choice.

There are lots of fancy decision-making frameworks out there, but my favorite is called the "gun test." I read about it in *The Achievement Habit*, a book by Stanford engineering professor Bernard Roth on applying the principles of design thinking to everyday life.[3]

Roth writes that when one of his students is wrestling with a big life decision (whether to attend grad school or take a job offer, for example), he points his fingers in the shape of a gun at the student's forehead and says, "OK, you have 15 seconds to decide or I'll pull the trigger. What's your decision?" According to Roth, everyone always knows the answer.

I especially like the language Roth uses to describe why the gun test is so effective: "Even if they do not ultimately take that path, this exercise usually releases the pressure built up around the decision-making process and gets them closer to a resolution." As I wrote for *Insider*, the point isn't really to choose one option or another. It's to realize that you *can* choose, and that you'll feel much freer afterward.[4]

Once you've done your due diligence—things like taking informational interviews with employees at the company where you'd like to work and bulking up your savings so that if a new project doesn't work out, you're not doomed—there's only so much you can know about where your decision will ultimately lead. Just pick something.

SUBPAR REASONS TO STAY IN A JOB YOU DON'T LIKE

As we learned in Chapter 2, it's critical to identify your motivations for sticking with a job you don't love. And that's not just to feel more confident about staying or to reconnect with your most important values. It's also a way to suss out whether you're staying for reasons that make sense. Because while there are plenty of good reasons to stay, there are also plenty of reasons you'll want to challenge.

Fear of Not Being "Gritty"

Since University of Pennsylvania professor Angela Duckworth (we met her in Chapter 3) took to the TED stage in 2013 to tell the world about the power of "grit," the construct itself has become something of a buzzword.[5] Duckworth defines grit as a combination of passion and perseverance, and says that individuals who measure high in grit tend to be more successful in the long term.

There are good reasons and questionable reasons to stay in a job you don't like. Make sure you know the difference.

But as we heard from Duckworth in Chapter 3, quitting your job doesn't necessarily indicate that you lack grit. Instead it might indicate that you've found a more effective way to achieve an important *career goal*, for example helping underserved students or holding people in power to account.

Recall that Duckworth advises people considering leaving their jobs to ask themselves what attracted them to this company in the first place. If your answer is something like, "This is what first attracted me in this direction, but actually this other company would be a better way for me to meet that goal," Duckworth said, then you should probably consider making the move. Staying in a company or a role that's not helping you meet the goal you've committed to isn't so gritty (or sensible) after all.

Even if you're not influenced by accounts of grit specifically, you may be worried that quitting your job is a sign that you're not hardworking or committed enough. In a *Refinery29* article published in 2021, clinical psychologist and author Ellen Hendriksen told Elizabeth Gulino that the fear of "being *labeled* a quitter" is rooted in the American "belief that anything can be accomplished through hard work."[6] And while hard work will generally push your career forward, there are limits to how much it can get you.

If you're one of those people who are consumed by this particular fear, I'd encourage you to consider the possibility that you're not a quitter all around. What if, instead, you saw yourself as someone who's able to perceive and seize opportunity?

The Sunk-Cost Fallacy

Quitting a job—especially one you've held for a while—can be scary. But staying in a job you're less than satisfied with just because you feel like you've already put so much time and effort into it may not serve you well.

Psychologists call this tendency falling prey to the "sunk-cost fallacy," and this cognitive bias often drives people's fears about quitting their job.[7] In other words, you feel you've wasted part of your career in this role and you can't get those years back, so you might as well continue here. This is the kind of thinking that it's certainly worth challenging, either on your own or in a conversation with a friend, family member, career coach, or therapist. You can try to identify *why* you think the last several years of your career must determine the rest of your professional life.

Guilt

Guilt is an incredibly common reason for staying in an unsatisfying job. Often people feel guilty about hating—and leaving—something stable and relatively lucrative, especially if it's the kind of work their parents would have killed for.

Recall Annafi Wahed, from Chapter 11, who ended up leaving her prestigious consulting job without telling her mother. Wahed knew her mother would be disappointed, since she brought Wahed to the United States hoping that Wahed would build a successful career and be able to take care of herself without relying on anyone else for support. Wahed was ashamed of feeling miserable at a job that allowed her to easily afford a one-bedroom New York City apartment of her own.

Similarly, Christine Cruzvergara, the Handshake executive we met in Chapter 2, told me that she's the daughter of two immigrants who made it clear that she should *never* quit a job without another one lined up, to avoid jeopardizing both her financial health and her ability to advance in her career. Cruzvergara therefore kept a job she didn't love and continued to excel in it, even while dedicating significant energy to networking and job searching. Maybe that was the right move for Cruzvergara at that time. But it was also exhausting.

This kind of guilt isn't exactly an illegitimate reason for staying in a job. Family influences can be strong, and whatever you're feeling right now is valid. But if your fears around disappointing your parents are keeping you stuck in a job that's contributing to your unhappiness, it's important to consider other options besides simply sticking it out forever.

To be sure, this strategy will involve some deep introspection. The goal is to come to terms with your fears and to clarify how much discomfort you're willing to tolerate for the sake of finding some more emotional freedom.

REMEMBER THIS

- Not everyone has the energy to change careers right now, and some people find things like professional networking loathsome instead of enlivening. That's OK.
- See if you can identify what exactly about quitting scares you. That extra clarity will help you make an informed career decision.
- Sometimes being "gritty" means leaving one job to take another that will better allow you to pursue a big goal.

TRY THIS

MAP YOUR CAREER VENN DIAGRAM

If you haven't already, evaluate your current job in the context of Patty McCord's three questions:

1. Is this what I love to do?
2. Is this what I'm extraordinarily good at doing?
3. Is this something the company needs someone to be great at?

Which questions did you answer no or not really to? Do you think your answers to those questions might become yes in the near future? If not, consider whether you'd be willing to make some kind of change—like switching jobs, bosses, or employers—so that your career situation is closer to the ideal.

CONCLUSION

THERE ARE NO WRONG CHOICES

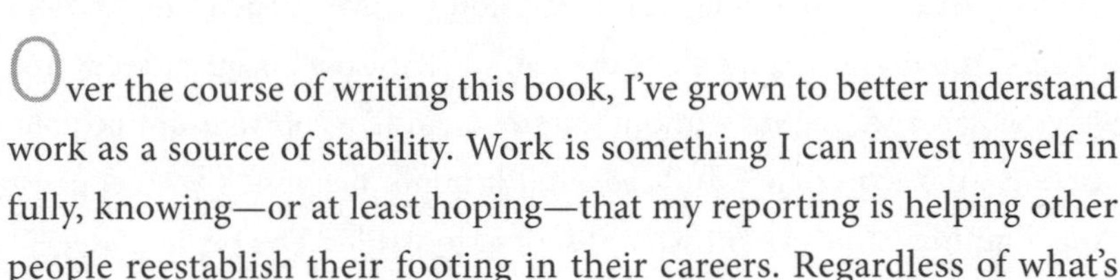

Over the course of writing this book, I've grown to better understand work as a source of stability. Work is something I can invest myself in fully, knowing—or at least hoping—that my reporting is helping other people reestablish their footing in their careers. Regardless of what's going on in my personal life, trying to keep up with the changing nature of jobs and careers gives me a strong sense of purpose and meaning.

At the same time, during the recent coronavirus pandemic, I sometimes resented my job in ways that weren't really fair and didn't make a lot of sense. On many, many days, I felt isolated and lonely, especially once my husband transitioned back to working in his office. I hadn't been to the *Insider* office in months, since both the commute from Queens to Manhattan and the workday itself would involve more potential exposure to the virus than I was comfortable with. Often, I projected those feelings onto my job—I told myself it wasn't interesting enough, it wasn't fun enough, and *that* was why I felt so frustrated.

Then I would take a step back and remember that it wasn't the *job* that was bothering me; it was the pandemic that had caused me and plenty of other professionals to cloister ourselves away.

None of this had happened when I first came up with the idea for this book. I knew that helping people feel less stuck in their careers was important—but the pandemic and the remote-work era have shown me just how central our relationship to work is in our lives. This is true even if nothing obviously disruptive happens in your career—no layoffs, no firings, no huge promotions. Work, whatever we're doing and whether we love it or not, gives our daily lives direction and purpose, even if we're not always feeling that.

And because most of us work every weekday, if not every day, it's easy to assume that every distressing feeling we experience is a function of our jobs. That if we're, say, bored or stressed, the best solution is to make a big and immediate change in our work lives. Work is alternately our friend and our foe; it both shapes who we are and reflects it.

Here's the optimal outcome I envision for every one of this book's readers: You're able to take stock of what work means to you and reevaluate your career decisions without judgment. You're able to examine your current work experience and see what it might become if you let go of your limiting beliefs about what it *should* look like. You begin to see all the different directions in which you might steer your career, instead of thinking things can either stay exactly as they are or change radically. And you feel a little bit less alone, both in your disappointment with your current career circumstance and in your striving for something better.

This book isn't designed to give you more agency in your career—you already have that. Instead I want you to start exercising some of that agency. Ideally, this book has helped you develop the skill of spotting pieces of your work experience that are within your locus of control and then seizing on them. Because, as we've learned in the past 12 chapters, much of it *is* in your control.

Some of these pieces are more about your mindset and your perception of what you're doing at work every day. Others are more readily tangible, like the tasks on your to-do list and the colleagues and clients you meet with regularly. Both areas are important and impactful—which one you tackle first depends largely on what you feel is missing from your work right now. And the sooner you internalize just how much discretion you have, the happier and more successful you'll be.

I do want to emphasize this: It doesn't mean you'll reach happily-ever-after status at work, at least not immediately. Work is never going to be perfect, as much as we wish it would be. Still, being able to identify what you have the power to change and improve can be incredibly freeing. Likewise, recognizing what you probably don't have the capacity to change means you can stop banging your metaphorical head against the wall.

I sincerely hope the tools and insights in this book will be relevant for a long time and for many generations of workers. But I happen to be writing this book at a moment when the "future of work" is attracting a lot of interest and attention. Everyone wants to know—and share an opinion—on whether corporate America will ever resume its prepandemic shape. It's yet unclear whether employers will start calling workers back to the office en masse, or whether widespread remote work has staying power. It's similarly unclear whether employers will stay as focused as they are now on big concepts like purpose and meaning.

Even as a reporter who covers the workplace, I can't answer these critical questions with any certainty. I do know that you have the potential to draft your own "future of work" plans, independent of where business leadership or the labor market is headed. It's a matter of getting to know yourself and the unique value you bring to an organization, then using that knowledge to map out the next phase of your career.

And remember: That next phase can hinge on a change like getting rid of a few annoying job tasks or letting go of the belief that if you're not rescuing people from burning buildings, your work is worthless. Feeling better about work is just as often about cutting yourself some slack or lowering your expectations as it is about pushing yourself to be more proactive or ambitious.

Thank you for coming on this journey with me. I hope it's left you feeling more empowered to articulate what you want—and then go for it.

There are no wrong choices—only endless possibilities.

RESOURCES I RECOMMEND

If you're looking to learn more about career development, I've listed below a series of resources that can guide you. Many of them have helped me in my career; others have helped my colleagues in theirs.

BOOKS

Designing Your Life: How to Build a Well-Lived, Joyful Life, by Bill Burnett and Dave Evans

I mentioned *Designing Your Life* earlier in this book because it contains so many nuggets of wisdom and strategic exercises to get unstuck. Burnett and Evans are professors of engineering at Stanford's d.school, and here they apply the principles of design thinking, a process typically used to improve an object or experience, to everyday life and work. I think often about tools like "Odyssey Planning," in which you map out different ways your life and career could unfold, because it shows how many options you really have. (And if you enjoy this book, check out the sequels: *Designing Your Work Life* and *Designing Your New Work Life*.)

The Ambition Decisions: What Women Know About Work, Family, and the Path to Building a Life, by Hana Schank and Elizabeth Wallace

Schank and Wallace are journalists and former college classmates, and when they published *The Ambition Decisions*, it had been more than two decades since they graduated. For the book, they interviewed several women from their sorority and highlighted common themes in how these women's lives and careers unfolded. I most appreciate how Schank and Wallace encourage readers to expand their definition of "ambitious," and to consider the various factors that both get in the way of and support women in achieving their biggest dreams.

The New Rules of Work: The Muse Playbook for Navigating the Modern Workplace, by Alexandra Cavoulacos and Kathryn Minshew

This book, by the president and CEO of the career advice site The Muse, was published in 2017, though I have a feeling its most important lessons will apply for a while. Cavoulacos and Minshew push readers to exercise the agency they have by thinking about their next career move in advance and seizing opportunities when they arise. For example, the authors recommend (and share templates for) emailing the hiring manager for a job you didn't get and letting the manager know you'd be interested in future openings. Likewise, the authors advise checking out listings for your dream job years ahead of time so you know which skills you still need to build. It's practical—and easy—advice to follow.

Off the Clock: Feel Less Busy While Getting More Done, by Laura Vanderkam

Vanderkam is a time management expert, and this book is one of several she's written to help readers reimagine their relationship to productivity. *Off the Clock* thrilled me with its "tricks" to really enjoy the time when you're not working, like prioritizing what your future self will cherish (an evening out with a friend) instead of indulging what your present self wants (an evening in with TV). Like all Vanderkam's books, this one advocates a very intentional approach to daily life and shows readers how to avoid squandering even one second.

The Power of Meaning: Crafting a Life That Matters, by Emily Esfahani Smith

Smith's book grew out of her viral article for *The Atlantic*, about how too many of us chase happiness over meaning in life when it should be the other way around. The book is a lovely compilation of case studies featuring all different kinds of people and professionals, who have found meaning in their lives. I especially liked Smith's portrait of the zoologist who couldn't imagine doing anything other than caring for and spending time with animals. *The Power of Meaning* will certainly prompt you to reconsider where and how you create meaning in your own life and career.

The First 90 Days: Proven Strategies for Getting Up to Speed Faster and Smarter, by Michael D. Watkins

My former colleague Karen Ho recommended this book by Watkins, a leadership development consultant to Fortune 500 companies. "It's great for when you're starting a new job, a new role, or just want to understand the importance of small and big choices in your career," Karen said.

The Goal: A Process of Ongoing Improvement, by Eliyahu M. Goldratt

Karen also recommended this bestselling business novel because "it helped me realize how many daily things I do are processes, how to identify weaknesses, and how to implement successful changes among teams over time."

Pivot: The Only Move That Matters Is Your Next One by Jenny Blake

My colleague Marguerite Ward, an *Insider* correspondent covering diversity and leadership, loved this guide to making a career change. So did I. *Pivot* was written by career coach and former Googler Jenny Blake. (I mentioned Blake's work earlier in this book.) Blake breaks down career changes into four phases that readers can follow systematically, whether they're trying to move into an entirely new industry or simply hoping to get a promotion. The most important thing to remember about Blake's approach is that even if you don't end up where you expected, you'll be better off professionally and personally for having gone through the pivot process.

The Memo: What Women of Color Need to Know to Secure a Seat at the Table, by Minda Harts

Marguerite recommended this book for women of color especially. Harts runs the career development platform The Memo LLC, and in her book *The Memo*, she draws on her experience as a corporate consultant. As Marguerite wrote for *Insider*, "Harts gives a first-hand, in-depth look at racism and sexism in the workplace, along with strategies women of color can employ to get the careers they deserve." Harts also "offers tips for managers and leaders who employ Black women and women of color so they are active allies," Marguerite wrote.

Mindset: The New Psychology of Success by Carol Dweck

Dweck is the Stanford University developmental psychologist who pioneered research on "growth mindset." Marguerite thinks every professional should read it—and I agree. (Dweck and growth mindset make an appearance in this book.) In *Mindset*, Dweck explains how her research led her to study differences between people who relish learning and challenges and those who are more wary of failure.

PODCASTS AND ONLINE COURSES

Women at Work, podcast from the *Harvard Business Review*

I look forward to a new *Women at Work* episode every week the way some people look forward to a new episode of their favorite Netflix series. The guests—business professors, consultants, and real women with real career dilemmas—are always fabulous, and the hosts are excellent at drawing them out. One of my favorite episodes focused on successfully making a life or career change during the pandemic.

The Anxious Achiever, podcast from the *Harvard Business Review*

My colleague Hana Alberts, *Insider*'s real estate editor, said she's hooked on this podcast from host Morra Aarons-Mele, the founder of the social impact agency Women Online. (Aarons-Mele appears in this book talking about the decision to pursue entrepreneurship.) Past episodes have featured guests such as Harvard Business School Amy Edmondson on psychological safety and politician Huma Abedin and explored topics including neurodiversity, setting boundaries, and burnout.

The Pay Check, podcast from Bloomberg

Karen said that host Rebecca Greenfield and her team at Bloomberg Equality "consistently cover employment issues from a smart, engaging approach." Past topics have included the gender pay gap, the US government's role in paying for childcare, and racial disparities in homeownership.

Hello Monday, podcast from LinkedIn

Even before the pandemic hit, *Hello Monday* was all about making the changing world of work easier to understand. Host Jessi Hempel brings on guests like burnout experts Emily Nagoski and Amelia Nagoski, designer and brand consultant Debbie Millman, and psychologist and executive coach Lisa Orbé-Austin, to hear their perspectives on crafting a fulfilling and purpose-driven career. The episodes are easy to listen to and consistently fascinating.

"The Neuroscience of Learning," online course on LinkedIn

My colleague Julia Pugachevsky, *Insider*'s education and personal development editor, took this class when she was trying to figure out next steps in her career a few years ago. The class introduces students to cutting-edge scientific research on the topic, and Julia said she liked how the field of educational technology "used psychology, design, and writing to create more engaging and accessible coursework."

COLUMNS AND NEWSLETTERS

Karla Miller's work advice column in the *Washington Post*

My colleague Rebecca Knight, an *Insider* correspondent covering the future of work, turns often to Miller's weekly column. Miller provides counsel on timely topics like making a career transition, navigating a tricky interview process, and handling conflict with colleagues.

Culture Study newsletter from Anne Helen Petersen

Petersen is one of the most thoughtful and thought-provoking writers on modern workplace dynamics. (Her two most recent books are *Can't Even*, about millennial burnout, and *Out of Office*, about remote work.) Hana recommended Petersen's newsletter (available through Substack) specifically for "her writings on the future of work and our relationship to it."

OTHER EXERCISES AND TOOLS

Values Card Sort

The purpose of the Values Card Sort is to identify what's most meaningful to you in your career and to start crafting a more fulfilling work life. You simply sort the cards so that the values are ranked in order of importance to you. The cards are available on a variety of websites.

The VIA Survey of Character Strengths

This 120-question free survey is designed to pinpoint your greatest strengths, based on research from positive psychologists. Examples include creativity, honesty, teamwork, and humor, and VIA provides a simple assessment of how you might use your strengths in your daily life and career.

"5 Warning Signs You're in a Toxic Workplace, and What to Do About It Before It Ruins Your Personal Life," *Insider*

Marguerite published this thorough checklist to help readers identify a toxic workplace—and get out of it. Signs include only people in power speaking up and lots of distrust and gossiping. You can find the full list here: https://www.businessinsider.com/how-to-know-if-your-job-is-a-toxic-workplace-psychologists.

NOTES

Chapter 1

1. Shana Lebowitz, "Most Americans Don't Want to Be the Boss—and They're Probably Better Off," *Insider*, December 10, 2015, https://www.businessinsider.com/most-americans-dont-want-to-be-managers-2015-12.
2. Kim Parker, Rachel Minkin, and Jesse Bennett, "Economic Fallout from COVID-19 Continues to Hit Lower-Income Americans the Hardest," Pew Research Center, September 24, 2020, https://www.pewresearch.org/social-trends/2020/09/24/economic-fallout-from-covid-19-continues-to-hit-lower-income-americans-the-hardest/.
3. Kevin Roose, "Welcome to the YOLO Economy," *New York Times*, April 21, 2021, https://www.nytimes.com/2021/04/21/technology/welcome-to-the-yolo-economy.html.
4. Hannah Towey, "They Switched from Banking to DJing and from Retail to Tech—Here's How 6 Workers Pivoted Careers amid the Great Resignation," *Insider*, November 14, 2021, https://www.businessinsider.com/people-share-how-they-career-pivot-changed-jobs-during-pandemic-2021-11.
5. Rebecca Knight, "The Pandemic Struck Gen Xers Right in the Middle of Their Peak Earning Years. It's Been to Their Advantage," *Insider*, October 6, 2021, https://www.businessinsider.com/gen-x-traits-millennial-yolo-career-post-covid-2021-6.
6. Kate Duffy, "Nearly 40% of Workers Would Consider Quitting if Their Bosses Made Them Return to the Office Full Time, a New Survey Shows," Insider, June 2, 2021, https://www.businessinsider.com/quit-job-flexible-remote-working-from-home-return-to-office-2021-6.
7. Aaron Weinman, Samantha Stokes, and Reed Alexander, "Morgan Stanley and Goldman Sachs Are Refreshing Their Benefits Packages amid Wall Street's War for Talent. Here's How 8 Big Banks Stack Up on Leave Policies, Retirement Matching, and More," *Insider*, December 16, 2021, https://www.businessinsider.com/bank-employee-benefits-paid-leave-retirement-matching-goldman-bofa-wells-2021-11.

Chapter 2

1. Bradley Saacks and Shana Lebowitz, "College Students Don't Want to Return in the Fall, and It Could Cause Many Universities to Collapse," *Insider*, May 21, 2020, https://www.businessinsider.com/presenting-us-higher-education-colleges-financial-struggles-pandemic-online-education-2020-5.
2. Melanie Hanson, "Student Loan Debt Statistics," Education Data Initiative, updated November 17, 2021, https://educationdata.org/student-loan-debt-statistics.
3. Jesse Rothstein and Cecilia Elena Rouse, "Constrained After College: Student Loans and Early-Career Occupational Choices," *Journal of Public Economics* 95, nos. 1–2 (February 2011): 149–163.
4. Martin Gervais and Nicolas L. Ziebarth, "Life After Debt: Post-Graduation Consequences of Federal Student Loans," *Journal of Economic Literature*, no. I22 (February 2017).
5. Mark Lino, "The Cost of Raising a Child," US Department of Agriculture, February 18, 2020, https://www.usda.gov/media/blog/2017/01/13/cost-raising-child.
6. Tasha Eurich, *Insight* (New York: Crown Business, 2017), 283.
7. Raven Molloy, Christopher Smith, and Abigail Wozniak, "Changing Stability in U.S. Employment Relationships: A Tale of Two Tails," National Bureau of Economic Research (February 2020).
8. Katherine McLaughlin, "A Millennial Lawyer Who Quit Her 6-Figure Job Without Another Lined Up Took 4 Steps First to Make Sure She Could Afford It," *Insider*, September 20, 2021, https://www.businessinsider.com/personal-finance/steps-lawyer-took-before-she-quit-her-job-2021-9.
9. Perri Ormont Blumberg, "I'm a 26-Year-Old Who Quit My 6-Figure Job at Deloitte to Be a TikToker and Coach. People Thought I Was Crazy, but I'm on Track to Match My Old Salary—Here's How I Did It," *Insider*, July 26, 2021, https://www.businessinsider.com/quit-6-figure-job-deloitte-consulting-start-coaching-business-tiktok-2021-7.
10. Dan P. McAdams, "American Identity: The Redemptive Self," 2007 *Division One Award Addresses* 43, no. 1 (Spring 2008): 20–27.
11. Ibid.
12. Kate C. McLean et al., "Redemptive Stories and Those Who Tell Them Are Preferred in the U.S.," *Collabra: Psychology* 1, no. 39 (2020).
13. Jonathan M. Adler, "Living into the Story: Agency and Coherence in a Longitudinal Study of Narrative Identity Development and Mental Health over the Course of Psychotherapy," *Journal of Personality and Social Psychology* 102, no. 2 (2012): 367–389.
14. "Your Best Employees Are Leaving. But Is It Personal or Practical?," Randstad, August 28, 2018, https://www.randstadusa.com/business/

business-insights/employee-retention/your-best-employees-are-leaving-it-personal-practical/.

Chapter 3

1. Lauren Mechling, "Career Coaching Today: Forget the Corporate Ladder and Find Yourself," *New York Times*, November 20, 2021, https://www.nytimes.com/2021/11/20/business/career-spiritual-coaching-pandemic html.
2. Shana Lebowitz, "I Went to a Career Coach So You Don't Have to—and It Was a Rude Awakening," *Insider*, April 14, 2020, https://www.businessinsider.com/should-i-use-a-career-coach-2017-7.
3. Kathryn Dill, "More People Quit to Take a New Job from an Old Boss," *Wall Street Journal*, December 15, 2021, https://www.wsj.com/articles/the-new-job-offer-you-want-could-come-from-your-old-boss-11639564205.
4. Aki Ito, "'Boomerang Employees' Who Quit During the Pandemic Are Starting to Ask for Their Old Jobs Back," *Insider*, October 14, 2021, https://www.businessinsider.com/job-market-hiring-trends-expect-boomerang-employees-labor-shortage-great-resignation.
5. Shana Lebowitz, "Netflix Encourages Employees to Interview at Other Companies—Here's Why," *Insider*, January 18, 2018, https://www.businessinsider.com/netflix-encourages-employees-to-interview-at-other-companies-2018-1.
6. Ibid.
7. Peter Flade, Jim Asplund, and Gwen Elliot, "Employees Who Use Their Strengths Outperform Those Who Don't," Gallup, October 8, 2015, https://www.gallup.com/workplace/236561/employees-strengths-outperform-don.aspx.
8. Kerri Twigg, *The Career Stories Method* (Page Two Books, 2021), 25.
9. Shana Lebowitz, "Here's When It's OK to Give Up on Your Job and Quit," *Insider*, May 5, 2016, https://www.businessinsider.com/angela-duckworth-when-its-ok-to-quit-your-job-2016-5.
10. Neil Irwin, *How to Win in a Winner-Take-All World* (New York: St. Martin's Press, 2019).
11. Shana Lebowitz, "Becoming a 'Big-Picture Thinker' Is One of the Best Ways to Succeed at Work," *Insider,* August 5, 2019, https://www.businessinsider.com/career-success-know-why-your-job-is-important-2019-8.
12. Shana Lebowitz, "The Worst Part of Your Workday Probably Happens Before You Even Get to the Office," *Insider*, April 24, 2017, https://www.businessinsider.com/commuting-is-terrible-2017-4.
13. Shana Lebowitz, "A Harvard Psychologist Reveals a Simple Trick for Getting over the Hardest Moments in Your Day," *Insider*, August 29, 2016, https://

www.businessinsider.com/harvard-psychologist-how-to-solve-problems-at-work-2016-8.

14. Bill Burnett and Dave Evans, *Designing Your Life: How to Build a Well-Lived, Joyful Life* (New York: Alfred A. Knopf, 2016).
15. Jenny Blake, *Pivot: The Only Move That Matters Is Your Next One* (New York: Portfolio/Penguin, 2016).
16. Shana Lebowitz, "This Brilliant Technique Is Less Gross Than Networking and Will Get You Actual Experience and Exposure," *Insider*, September 22, 2016, https://www.businessinsider.com/career-coach-and-former-googler-less-gross-alternative-to-networking-drafting-2016-9.
17. Shana Lebowitz, "Stanford Professors Explain Their Best Strategy to Figure Out Whether You Should Leave Your Job," *Insider*, October 11, 2016, https://www.businessinsider.com/should-i-leave-my-job-2016-10.

Chapter 4

1. Lindsay Gordon, "It's OK to Have a Boring Job," *Medium*, August 6, 2018, https://medium.com/@coaching_83940/its-ok-to-have-a-boring-job-23902b135699.
2. Rachel Montañez, "Want to Make a Career Change? Here's How and Why 3 Medical Doctors Did It," *Forbes*, July 21, 2020, https://www.forbes.com/sites/rachelmontanez/2020/07/21/want-to-make-a-career-change-heres-how-and-why-3-medical-doctors-did-it/?sh=6d11c46597c6.
3. William Wan, "Burned Out by the Pandemic, 3 in 10 Health-Care Workers Consider Leaving the Profession," *Washington Post*, April 22, 2021, https://www.washingtonpost.com/health/2021/04/22/health-workers-covid-quit/.
4. Shawn Achor, Andrew Reece, Gabriella Rosen Kellerman, and Alexi Robichaux, "9 out of 10 People Are Willing to Earn Less Money to Do More-Meaningful Work," *Harvard Business Review*, November 6, 2018, https://hbr.org/2018/11/9-out-of-10-people-are-willing-to-earn-less-money-to-do-more-meaningful-work.
5. Erin Griffith, "Why Are Young People Pretending to Love Work?" *New York Times*, January 26, 2019, https://www.nytimes.com/2019/01/26/business/against-hustle-culture-rise-and-grind-tgim.html.
6. Derek Thompson, "Workism Is Making Americans Miserable," *The Atlantic*, February 24, 2019, https://www.theatlantic.com/ideas/archive/2019/02/religion-workism-making-americans-miserable/583441/.
7. Juliana Kaplan and Madison Hoff, "Over 90% of Job Switchers Said They Quit Because the Pandemic Made Them Feel like 'Life Is Too Short to Stay in a Job They Weren't Passionate About,'" *Insider*, December 2, 2021, https://www.businessinsider.com/why-workers-quit-pandemic-showed-life-too-short-great-resignation-2021-11.

8. Katie Johnston, "'I Want to Do the Things That Matter to Me': Pandemic Spurs Search for Jobs with Purpose," *Boston Globe*, May 10, 2021, https://www.bostonglobe.com/2021/05/10/business/i-want-do-things-that-matter-me-pandemic-spurs-search-jobs-with-purpose/.
9. Jennifer Levitz, "Covid-19 Was a Wake-Up Call, Leading Many to Make Lifestyle and Career Changes," *Wall Street Journal*, April 11, 2021, https://www.wsj.com/articles/covid-19-was-a-wake-up-call-leading-many-to-make-lifestyle-and-career-changes-11618133400?mod=article_inline.
10. Shana Lebowitz, "How to Find Meaning if You've Lost Your Job and Are Struggling with an Identity Crisis," *Insider*, 2018, updated June 2, 2020, https://www.businessinsider.com/meaningful-work-job-satisfaction-2019-3.
11. Adam M. Grant, "The Significance of Task Significance: Job Performance Effects, Relational Mechanisms, and Boundary Conditions," *Journal of Applied Psychology* 93, no. 1 (2008): 108–124.
12. Ryan W. Buell, Tami Kim, and Chia-Jung Tsay, "Creating Reciprocal Value Through Operational Transparency," *Management Science* 63, no. 6 (June 2017) 1673–1695.
13. Jochen I. Menges, Danielle V. Tussing, Andreas Wihler, and Adam Grant, "When Job Performance Is All Relative: How Family Motivation Energizes Effort and Compensates for Intrinsic Motivation," *Academy of Management Journal* 60, no. 2 (February 2016).
14. Kerri Twigg, *The Career Stories Method* (Page Two Books, 2021), 55.
15. Lindsay Gordon, "Why Is There Only One Option for Contribution in Your Job?" LinkedIn, October 7, 2021, https://www.linkedin.com/pulse/why-only-one-option-contribution-your-job-lindsay-gordon/.

Chapter 5

1. Patricia Chen, Phoebe C. Ellsworth, and Norbert Schwarz, "Finding a Fit or Developing It: Implicit Theories About Achieving Passion for Work," *Personality and Social Psychology Bulletin* 41, no. 10 (July 2015): 1411–1424.
2. For some insight into cross-cultural differences around fit and develop mindsets, see Paul A. O'Keefe, E. Horberg, Patricia Chen, and Krishna Savani, "Should You Pursue Your Passions as a Career? Cultural Differences in the Emphasis on Passion in Career Decisions," *Journal of Organizational Behavior* (July 2021).
3. Patricia Chen and Phoebe C. Ellsworth, "Lay Theories of How Passion for Work Is Achieved," in Robert J. Vallerand and Nathalie Houlfort (eds.), *Passion for Work: Theory, Research, and Applications* (New York: Oxford University Press, 2019), 154.

Chapter 6

1. Patricia Chen et al., "A Strategic Mindset: An Orientation Toward Strategic Behavior During Goal Pursuit," *Proceedings of the National Academy of Sciences of the United States of America* 117, no. 25 (June 2020): 14066–14072.
2. Drake Baer, "How Your Mindset Determines Your Success, Well-Being, and Love Life," *Insider*, August 20, 2014, https://www.businessinsider.com/how-a-growth-mindset-leads-to-success-2014-8.
3. Shana Lebowitz, "People Can't Stop Talking About Counterintuitive Advice for Being a Good Boss," *Insider*, February 1, 2018, https://www.businessinsider.com/management-advice-dont-answer-employee-questions-immediately-2018-1.
4. Susan David, *Emotional Agility: Get Unstuck, Embrace Change, and Thrive in Work and Life* (New York: Avery, 2016), 208.
5. Melody Wilding, *Trust Yourself* (San Francisco: Chronicle Prism, 2021).

Chapter 7

1. Shana Lebowitz, "How to Turn a Boring Job into a Meaningful Career," *Insider*, December 1, 2015, https://www.businessinsider.com/turn-a-boring-job-into-a-meaningful-career-job-crafting-2015-12.
2. Amy Wrzesniewski and Jane Dutton, "Crafting a Job: Revisioning Employees as Active Crafters of Their Work," *Academy of Management Review* 26, no. 2 (April 2001).
3. Jane E. Dutton and Amy Wrzesniewski, "What Job Crafting Looks Like," *Harvard Business Review*, March 12, 2020, https://hbr.org/2020/03/what-job-crafting-looks-like.
4. Aki Ito, "Work from Home Is Going to Change How You Get Promoted, and Why," *Insider*, November 1, 2021, https://www.businessinsider.com/work-from-home-performance-evaluations-management-reviews-promotions-raises.
5. Erica Volini, Kraig Eaton, and David Mallon, "The Worker-Employer Relationship Disrupted," *Deloitte Insights*, July 21, 2021, https://www2.deloitte.com/us/en/insights/focus/human-capital-trends/2021/the-evolving-employer-employee-relationship.html.
6. Ito, "Work from Home."
7. Shana Lebowitz, "A Former Googler and Facebook Exec Says Asking Your Boss This Simple Question When You Start a New Job Is The Best Way to Ensure Success from the Get-Go," *Insider*, updated May 6, 2019, https://www.businessinsider.com/what-to-do-when-you-start-a-new-job-2018-9.

Chapter 8

1. Hayley Peterson, "Inside Sears' Death Spiral: How an Iconic American Brand Has Been Driven to the Edge of Bankruptcy," *Insider*, January 8, 2017, https://www.businessinsider.com/sears-failing-stores-closing-edward-lampert-bankruptcy-chances-2017-1.
2. Shana Lebowitz, "'We Are the Band on the *Titanic*': The Former HR Chief at Sears Shares How He Kept His Team Focused and Motivated During the Retailer's Historic Implosion," *Insider*, October 6, 2019, https://www.businessinsider.com/sears-former-hr-chief-dean-carter-patagonia-career-advice.
3. Shana Lebowitz, "The Onetime HR Chiefs of Google and Goldman Sachs Are Betting on Surging Demand for Diversity-and-Inclusion Tech. Here's Their Plan for Remaking the $148 Billion Market," *Insider*, July 2, 2020, https://www.businessinsider.com/google-goldman-sachs-former-hr-chiefs-quantify-diversity-inclusion-culture-2020-6.
4. Shana Lebowitz, "How to Make a Drastic Career Change, from an Executive Coach Who's Helped Countless People Unhappy at Work," *Insider*, updated August 18, 2020, https://www.businessinsider.com/job-search-advice-dont-change-industry-function-at-same-time-2018-9.
5. Shana Lebowitz and Weng Cheong, "Microsoft, Mondelez, and Canada Goose Look for People Who Thrive amid Constant Change. Here's How They Measure Adaptability in Job Candidates—and How to Know if You Fit the Bill," *Insider*, February 3, 2020, https://www.businessinsider.com/how-hiring-managers-measure-adaptability-job-candidates-2020-1.
6. Shana Lebowitz and Ebony Flake, "A Few Small Changes Can Make You Happier at a Job You Don't Like, Experts Say," *Insider*, Updated November 26, 2021, https://www.businessinsider.com/how-to-be-happier-at-a-job-you-dont-like-2021-7.
7. Hana Schank and Elizabeth Wallace, *The Ambition Decisions: What Women Know About Work, Family, and the Path to Building a Life* (New York: Viking, 2018).
8. Brian J. Brim, "How a Focus on People's Strengths Increases Their Work Engagement," Gallup, May 2, 2019, https://www.gallup.com/workplace/242096/focus-people-strengths-increases-work-engagement.aspx.
9. Shana Lebowitz, "The HR Chief of an $18 Billion Holding Company with Brands like Vimeo and Daily Beast Started Out as an Executive Assistant. Here Are the 3 Steps She Took to Get There," *Insider*, May 27, 2019, https://www.businessinsider.com/career-advice-new-job-hr-chief-iac-2019-5.
10. Laura Morgan Roberts et al., "How to Play to Your Strengths," *Harvard Business Review*, January 2005, https://hbr.org/2005/01/how-to-play-to-your-strengths.
11. Shana Lebowitz, "Goldman Sachs' Outgoing Talent Chief Shares the 3 Questions He Asks Himself Before Taking Any New Role—Including His

Next One as CEO of a HR Tech Startup," *Insider*, November 3, 2019, https://www.businessinsider.com/career-advice-goldman-sachs-dane-holmes-how-to-choose-job-2019-10.

12. Shana Lebowitz, "Goldman Sachs' Head of HR Says an 'Underrated' Factor Should Make a Big Difference in Which Job You Choose—Especially if You're Going to Be Logging Long Hours," *Insider*, September 14, 2018.
13. Teresa Amabile and Steven Kramer, *The Progress Principle: Using Small Wins to Ignite Joy, Engagement, and Creativity at Work* (Boston: Harvard Business Review Press, 2011), 20.

Chapter 9

1. Tom Peters, "The Brand Called You," *Fast Company*, August 31, 1997, https://www.fastcompany.com/28905/brand-called-you.
2. Wendy Marx, "A Personal Branding Expert Shares What It Takes to Build a Successful Reputation," *Fast Company*, February 3, 2021, https://www.fastcompany.com/90600522/a-personal-branding-expert-shares-what-it-takes-to-build-a-successful-reputation.
3. Jennifer Ortakales Dawkins and Shana Lebowitz, "A BET Executive Used Self-Advocacy to Advance Her Career, Sending Emails to Her Boss' Boss. Here's How She Says to Make Yourself Stand Out," *Insider*, February 20, 2020, https://www.businessinsider.com/how-to-outline-your-accomplishments-email-boss-promotion-raise-2020-2.
4. Roy Maurer, "2021 Recruiting Trends Shaped by the Pandemic," SHRM Talent Acquisition, February 1, 2021, https://www.shrm.org/resourcesandtools/hr-topics/talent-acquisition/pages/2021-recruiting-trends-shaped-by-covid-19.aspx.
5. Shana Lebowitz, "There's a Golden Opportunity for Entrepreneurs to Break into the $76.4 Billion Edtech Market," *Insider*, November 25, 2020; https://www.businessinsider.com/business-opportunities-entrepreneurs-startups-workforce-education-technology-retraining-skills-gap-2020-11.
6. LinkedIn provided me with a list of employers' career development programs in November 2021 from which I selected these examples.
7. Gopika Maya Santhosh, "Where Internal Mobility Is Most Common Since COVID-19: Top Countries, Industries, and Jobs," *LinkedIn Talent Blog*, October 28, 2020, https://www.linkedin.com/business/talent/blog/talent-strategy/where-internal-mobility-is-most-common.
8. Shana Lebowitz, "Google and Facebook Let Employees Try Different Jobs and Teams. Here's How Any Company Can Use This Strategy to Keep High Performers from Getting Bored and Quitting," *Insider*, updated January 22, 2020, https://www.businessinsider.com/companies-employees-change-jobs-internal-mobility-2018-12.

9. Shana Lebowitz, "Mastercard's HR Chief Says the Company Has Fast-Tracked the Careers of Hundreds of Employees During the Recession. Here's a Look Inside the Program," *Insider*, September 22, 2020, https://www.businessinsider.com/mastercard-project-possible-pandemic-recession-career-development-opportunities-internal-mobility-2020-9.
10. Suman Bhattacharyya, "How the Covid-19 Pandemic Changed Employee Training," *Wall Street Journal*, updated November 27, 2021, https://www.wsj.com/articles/how-covid19-changed-employee-training-11637612390.
11. Aman Kidwai, "Inside Unilever's Program That Allows Employees to Try Out New Jobs and Gig Working Opportunities at the Company," *Insider*, May 5, 2021, https://www.businessinsider.com/unilever-program-allowing-employees-try-out-new-jobs-gig-working-2021-5.
12. Shana Lebowitz, "Booz Allen Hamilton's HR Chief Reveals the Question She Asks Job Candidates to See if They're Invested in Their Career. Here's What She Wants to Hear in Response," *Insider*, September 17, 2020, https://www.businessinsider.com/booz-allen-hamilton-hiring-hr-chief-job-interview-question-proactivity-2020-9.
13. Guy Berger, "How to Become an Executive," LinkedIn, September 9, 2016, https://www.linkedin.com/pulse/how-become-executive-guy-berger-ph-d-/?published=t.
14. Shana Lebowitz, "A Former Googler and Facebook Exec Says Your Parents' Career Path Is Just About Dead, and There's a Better Way to Move Up in the World," *Insider*, October 2, 2018, https://www.businessinsider.com/career-ladder-dead-former-facebook-executive-2018-10.
15. Ibid.
16. Shana Lebowitz, "From IKEA to Home Depot, Major Companies Are Offering 'Intrapreneurship' Programs That Let Top Talent Lead Their Own Startup-Like Projects. Here's How They Work," *Insider*, updated May 15, 2019, https://www.businessinsider.com/home-depot-ikea-accenture-corporate-innovation-labs-2018-9.
17. Tomas Chamorro-Premuzic, "Why You Should Become an 'Intrapreneur,'" *Harvard Business Review*, March 26, 2020, https://hbr.org/2020/03/why-you-should-become-an-intrapreneur.
18. Dominick Reuter, "How to Know Which of the 5 Entrepreneur Types You Are, Based on Your Goals and the Risks You're Willing to Take," *Insider*, updated August 6, 2020, https://www.businessinsider.com/how-to-know-which-of-5-entrepreneur-types-you-are.
19. Jason C. Gawke, Marjan J. Gorgievski, and Arnold B. Bakker, "Employee Intrapreneurship and Work Engagement: A Latent Change Score Approach," *Journal of Vocational Behavior* 100 (2017): 88–100.
20. Becky Wood, "The Pandemic Made Bad Managers Even Worse in These Three Areas," *Humu Insights*, October 25, 2021, https://www.humu.com/blog/the-pandemic-made-bad-managers-even-worse-in-these-three-areas.

21. Caroline Hroncich, "Most Bosses Think They're Doing a Better Job Leading Than They Actually Are. Here Are Some Ways to Close the Gap," *Insider*, October 19, 2020, https://www.businessinsider.com/employees-managers-pandemic-leadership-struggles-2020-10.
22. Stefanie Tignor, "Can a Bad Manager Make You Like Your Job . . . More?," *Humu Insights*, April 23, 2019, https://www.humu.com/blog/can-a-bad-manager-make-you-like-your-job-more.

Chapter 10

1. Shana Lebowitz, "Super-Successful People like Warren Buffett and Marissa Mayer Swear by Their Hobbies, So I Spent a Month Trying to Find One of My Own," *Insider*, August 5, 2018, https://www.businessinsider.com/hobbies-make-you-less-boring-person-2018-7.
2. Laura Vanderkam, *The New Corner Office: How the Most Successful People Work from Home* (New York: Portfolio/Penguin, 2020).
3. "The State of American Jobs," Pew Research Center, October 6, 2016, https://www.pewresearch.org/social-trends/2016/10/06/3-how-americans-view-their-jobs/.
4. Juliana Kaplan, "Fewer Adults See Their Job as a Source of Life's Meaning, and It Shows How the Pandemic Has Changed America's Relationship with Work," *Insider*, November 18, 2021, https://www.businessinsider.com/fewer-americans-see-work-source-meaning-labor-shortages-2021-11.
5. Eli Finkel, *The All-or-Nothing Marriage: How the Best Marriages Work* (New York: Dutton, 2017).
6. Shana Lebowitz, "A Psychologist Shares 3 Proven Strategies to Help You Work Through Conflict and Improve a Rocky Relationship," *Insider*, updated October 2, 2020, https://www.businessinsider.com/marriage-advice-relationship-expert-2018-5.
7. Sarah Green Carmichael, "The Research is Clear: Long Hours Backfire for People and for Companies," *Harvard Business Review*, August 19, 2015, https://hbr.org/2015/08/the-research-is-clear-long-hours-backfire-for-people-and-for-companies.
8. Mark Matousek, "Elon Musk Says People Need to Work Around 80 Hours per Week to Change the World," *Insider*, November 26, 2018, https://www.businessinsider.com/elon-musk-says-80-hours-per-week-needed-change-the-world-2018-11.
9. Eugene Kim, "Yahoo CEO Marissa Mayer Explains How She Worked 130 Hours a Week and Why It Matters," *Insider*, August 4, 2016, https://www.businessinsider.com/yahoo-ceo-marissa-mayer-on-130-hour-work-weeks-2016-8.

10. Rachel Feintzeig, "Burned Out? Maybe You Should Care Less About Your Job," *Wall Street Journal*, October 4, 2021, https://www.wsj.com/articles/burned-out-maybe-you-should-care-less-about-your-job-11633320061.
11. Stewart D. Friedman, "Get More Done by Focusing Less on Work," *Harvard Business Review*, February 5, 2015, https://hbr.org/2015/02/get-more-done-by-focusing-less-on-work.html.
12. Stewart D. Friedman, *Total Leadership* (Boston: Harvard Business Press, 2008).

Chapter 11

1. It's possible to take naltrexone long term. At the time of our interview, Hunt-Glassman had been on the medication for four years.
2. Shana Lebowitz, "Keep Your Day Job, Move Slowly, and Don't Worry About Building a Unicorn: A New York 'Startup School' Eschews Everything Silicon Valley Ever Preached," *Insider*, October 14, 2018, https://www.businessinsider.com/how-to-start-a-business-dont-quit-your-day-job-tacklebox-accelerator-2018-10.
3. Ibid.
4. Joseph Raffiee and Jie Feng, "Should I Quit My Day Job? A Hybrid Path to Entrepreneurship," *Academy of Management Journal* 57, no. 4 (2013).
5. Pierre Azoulay, Benjamin F. Jones, J. Daniel Kim, and Javier Miranda, "Research: The Average Age of a Successful Startup Founder Is 45," *Harvard Business Review*, July 11, 2018, https://hbr.org/2018/07/research-the-average-age-of-a-successful-startup-founder-is-45.
6. Josh Mitchell and Kathryn Dill, "Workers Quit Jobs in Droves to Become Their Own Bosses," *Wall Street Journal*, November 29, 2021, https://www.wsj.com/articles/workers-quit-jobs-in-droves-to-become-their-own-bosses-11638199199.
7. Keith Speitz, "What Percentage of Businesses Fail in Their First Year?," *Motley Fool*, updated May 16, 2017, https://www.fool.com/careers/2017/05/03/what-percentage-of-businesses-fail-in-their-first.aspx.
8. Shana Lebowitz, "The Ultimate Guide to Figuring Out How (and if) You Should Start Your Own Company," *Insider*, updated September 21, 2020, https://www.businessinsider.com/should-i-start-a-business-questions-to-ask-yourself-2019-5.
9. Áine Cain, "A Former Googler Who Left After 2 Years to Build Her Own Startup Explains How to Know It's Time to Quit Your Job," *Insider*, February 21, 2018, https://www.businessinsider.com/when-to-leave-job-ex-googler-2018-2.
10. Shana Lebowitz and Max Jungreis, "The Glitz of 'Entrepreneurship Porn' Leads Startup Founders to Make Fatal Business Mistakes. Here's How to

Avoid Them," *Insider*, updated October 27, 2020, https://www.business insider.com/starting-business-entrepreneurship-hard-7.

11. Morra Aarons-Mele, "The Dangerous Rise of 'Entrepreneurship Porn,'" *Harvard Business Review*, January 6, 2014, https://hbr.org/2014/01/the -dangerous-rise-of-entrepreneurship-porn.

Chapter 12

1. Patty McCord, *Powerful: Building a Culture of Freedom and Responsibility* (Silicon Guild, 2017).
2. Shana Lebowitz and Sherin Shibu, "A Former Y Combinator Partner Shares the Questions He Uses to Evaluate All Risks—Including Dropping out of Law School to Start His Own Business," *Insider*, updated September 17, 2019, https://www.businessinsider.com/former-y-combinator-partner -decided-to-drop-out-of-law-school-2018-10.
3. Bernard Roth, *The Achievement Habit: Stop Wishing, Start Doing, and Take Command of Your Life* (New York: Harper Business, 2015).
4. Shana Lebowitz, "A Stanford Professor Says the 'Gun Test' Can Help You Make Big Decisions," *Insider*, February 5, 2016, https://www.businessinsider .com/stanford-professor-gun-test-to-make-big-decisions-2016-2.
5. Angela Duckworth, "Grit: The Power of Passion and Perseverance," *TED Talks Education*, April 2013, https://www.ted.com/talks/angela_lee_g_grit_ the_power_of_passion_and_perseverance.
6. Elizabeth Gulino, "Why Quitting Is Good Actually," *Refinery29*, updated November 1, 2021, https://www.refinery29.com/en-us/how-to-quit-sunk -cost-fallacy-explained.
7. Ibid.

ACKNOWLEDGMENTS

This book grew directly out of my reporting for *Insider*, and so I owe tremendous gratitude to my managers and colleagues there. Thank you to Libby Kane, my unofficial mentor and official editor for several years, for inspiring me to find and tell stories about what it really means to have a job and a career today. Libby was also the very first person with whom I shared the idea for this book, and I'll never forget her words of encouragement. Thank you to Drake Baer, *Insider*'s unimaginably talented editor-at-large, for sponsoring this book—and me—even when I wasn't sure he should. To many other *Insider* compatriots who read proto-proposals and early drafts of this book—including Joel Marino, Caroline Hroncich, and Rebecca Knight—thank you for sharing your wisdom and for believing that a mashup of ideas in a Google Doc had the potential to be something more. Thanks, too, to my former *Insider* colleague and brilliant storyteller Dan Bobkoff, for hearing a kernel of something compelling in my ramblings about a book that could help people feel less stuck. Thank you to my agent, Carol Mann, for being excited about this book idea from the get-go and for patiently guiding me through the editorial process. And to my fabulous editor at McGraw Hill, Cheryl Segura, I'm delighted to be your partner in this adventure. To my book coach, Debbie Weil, I don't think I would have finished this book without your guidance, so thank you for helping me shape each chapter into something bigger and better. I'm equally thankful for my friends with experience in book publishing, especially Monica Palenzuela and Julie Perry, who fielded near-constant questions about how this whole thing works. Thanks to all who kindly spent a Saturday afternoon in a job-crafting workshop so I could write about it, and to my friends who let me interrogate them about the emotional piece of their careers so I could write about that, too. To Jason Gray, thank you for 16 years (and counting) of friendship of the heart. This book is so much stronger for your careful feedback, criticism, and ability to see the big picture. To Evan Green-Lowe, who I sometimes think knows me and what I'm trying to say better than I do: Thank you for supporting and challenging me, while I was writing this book and always. Thank you to my Brandeis women for your energy and enthusiasm, not to mention your emotional support—especially Jenna Brofsky and Lital Nada, who have carried me through the low points and helped me celebrate and appreciate the high ones. To every single person who shared their career story: Thank you for trusting me. Even the narratives that didn't make it into the final draft informed the advice and observations in this book. Thank you to my in-laws, Andrea, David, and Noah, for believing in me and my ambitions, and for welcoming me into the family from day one. Thanks to my little brother, Jay Lebowitz, for listening to his big sister's ideas even when they aren't that interesting, and for sharing his own, which always are. Thanks to my dad, Jeff Lebowitz, for opening his heart to me 33 years ago and never closing it. To my beautiful mom, Joan Lebowitz, thank you for being my role model, my best friend, and my heroine—the next book from this family will have your name on it. To my husband, Aaron Gaynor, thank you for holding my hand. I love you more every day. And to my son, Eli, who grew and danced inside me as I wrote this book: You're it.

INDEX

ABOUT THE AUTHOR

Photo credit: Kena Betancur.

SHANA LEBOWITZ GAYNOR is a journalist covering careers and the workplace. She has spent the past seven years at *Insider*, where she helped launch the HR Insider column and is now a correspondent reporting on leadership and the future of work. Her favorite projects to date include an exploration of gender and racial dynamics within the human resources industry, an analysis on burnout among US workers, and interviews with talent chiefs at Microsoft and Salesforce. Lebowitz Gaynor graduated from Brandeis University with a bachelor's degree in English and psychology and received a master's degree in English and comparative literature from Columbia University. She enjoys novels, snacks, and sunny days that permit the consumption of both. She lives in her hometown Queens, New York, with her husband and son. This is her first book.